How to End Family Policing

How to End Family Policing

From Outrage to Action

Edited by Erin Miles Cloud, Erica R. Meiners,
Shannon Perez-Darby, and C. Hope Tolliver

Haymarket Books
Chicago, Illinois

© 2025 Erin Miles Cloud, Erica R. Meiners, Shannon Perez-Darby, and C. Hope Tolliver

Published in 2025 by
Haymarket Books
P.O. Box 180165
Chicago, IL 60618
www.haymarketbooks.org

ISBN: 979-8-88890-456-5

Distributed to the trade in the US through Consortium Book Sales and Distribution (www.cbsd.com) and internationally through Ingram Publisher Services International (www.ingramcontent.com).

This book was published with the generous support of Lannan Foundation, Wallace Action Fund, and Marguerite Casey Foundation.

Special discounts are available for bulk purchases by organizations and institutions. Please email info@haymarketbooks.org for more information.

Cover artwork by Sam Kirk.
Cover and interior design by Eric Kerl.

Printed in Canada by union labor.

Library of Congress Cataloging-in-Publication data is available.
Library of Congress Control Number: 2025942967

10 9 8 7 6 5 4 3 2 1

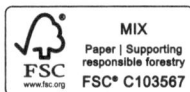

For and with all who have survived family policing
and built freedom and joy along the way

Contents

Action

Introduction

From Outrage to Action

Child welfare—How can this be wrong?
Don't children need to be protected?

Stories highlighting the value of child welfare systems recirculate across mainstream media outlets and water coolers: A few children might be unnecessarily assigned to a caseworker. Or a handful of caregivers, often mothers, might be investigated for allegations that prove false. But the overall outcome justifies these rare times when the system overreaches. Child safety, of course, is nonnegotiable. And besides, what else can be done? Don't you want to protect kids? And it is always better to be safe than sorry . . .

While this is the too familiar public script, our lives—C. Hope's, Erin's, Erica's, and Shannon's—highlight the lie at the core of what has been called child welfare but is actually the family policing system:

> We stand between the kindergarten teacher and our
> beautiful and brilliant sister, knowing that, on paper, this
> meeting is about supporting a child's educational pathway,

1

but hyperaware of the teacher's unspoken assessments of our sister—her scarred arms, dead tooth, gauntness. We know this teacher can trigger a chain of events that could remove this beloved child from our orbit because of potential parental unfitness.

We hold the deep trust of a young person who shares with us their experience of struggling to survive and to heal from sexual violence perpetrated by an intimate family member. Yet we teeter. We are legally bound to report this harm, but we know—intimately—that doing so will thrust this young person into a system that will do more harm and does not have the capacity to support this young person's decisions about their body and their healing pathway.

We answer the phone—at 5 a.m., 11 p.m., 3 p.m.—a call from a panicked loved one, a friend of a friend, a client, a neighbor, a cousin. A social worker was just at their door. In their hospital room. Asking questions at their child's school. The voice is rushed and reedy with anxiety. I don't know what is happening. Will I lose my daughter? Will I lose my job?

We cry/laugh, surrounded by our bio-family at our uncle's funeral, reminded of a core fact: Every one of our mother's ten siblings experienced investigations by child welfare services. And in none of these cases did these investigations and the resulting actions make our lives, or the lives of our cousins and our aunts/uncles, safer or better.

Our lives are hardly unique. So many Black, queer, noncitizen, Indigenous, poor, disabled, and/or Latinx people—particularly women—have overlapping and ongoing experiences of deep harm from these punitive systems. Panic surrounding an investigation. Confusion and anxiety after being thrust into state systems that hold violent power. Alarm when interfacing with caseworkers whose mouths sometimes say "support" but who, in reality, enact surveillance and policing. Trauma from forced removals and equally harmful placements. Perhaps the family of origin was a site of harm, but the state's response was as bad or worse—group and foster homes are often rife with violence. Resources always seem to flow for people to teach mandated parenting classes, caseworkers to inspect apartments, and lawyers to interview children—but not for rent, health care, childcare, food, or vacations.

Yes, young people experience violence, including gender and sexual harm. We take safety seriously and assert—with outrage—that the systems and services that purport to protect children actually make our communities less safe, more precarious. The very real forms of the worst of violence experienced by young people—particularly gender and sexual violence—are the repeated justifications for the consolidation and expansion of carceral or punitive logics. Far from protecting young people or resourcing care networks, all the tentacles of these punishing systems—for example, invasive investigations by social service agency staff, which can trigger enormous consequences and open registries that are held by the state and contain the names of anyone alleged to have committed or convicted of child neglect or harm—do not create safer communities. These punishing systems distract us from asking core questions: What *does* make our communities stronger and safer? How can we respond to the different needs of specific communities and individuals without privileging some over others—for example, by championing the specific needs of young people in ways that may directly jeopardize the adults in their lives? And, of course, as childhood and youth are fluid and temporary life stages, why create systems and policies that may eventually be used to punish the very people we purport to protect?

Our decades of shared organizing, study, and lived experiences repeatedly remind us that the criminal legal system cannot build safety. How to end the family policing system? *We must move from outrage to action*, and this book, with stories of harm and examples of forms of resistance and experimentation, is one contribution.

Outrage

Child welfare systems and institutions are persistently represented as beneficent and race-neutral public programs to help all children in need. This myth hides the violence the system generates and pollutes public policy and interpersonal norms and practices. Budgets balloon for investigations into allegations of neglect and harm, while the meager funding available for antipoverty or childcare programs always seems to shrink. Mandated reporter laws requiring people to criminally report suspected child neglect or abuse expand with deepening threats of criminal prosecution for those who fail to notify state agencies of their "suspicions." Child welfare is routinely weaponized against specific groups, in this moment particularly against people who are queer and/or transgender. Perhaps it is always a safe political move for policymakers to enact legislation and create new structures that profess to save the children. Yet far from creating safety, these components of the carceral or punitive state—including registries, investigations, and caregiver surveillance—deepen vulnerability and cause harm.

National statistics highlight what is often named as "racial disproportionality," yet these numbers demonstrate that white supremacy is embedded in these harmful state systems:

- While Black children make up only 14 percent of the child population in the United States, Black children are almost a quarter of the total population in foster care.[1]
- In the United States, 53 percent of all Black children will experience a child protective services investigation before the age of eighteen.[2]

State and local data also reveal deep injustices:

- In New York City, 90 percent of reports made to child protective services involve Black or Latinx children.[3]
- In Los Angeles, 19 percent of youth in the foster care system identify as LGBTQ (95 percent of the youth in foster care are also non-white).[4]
- In Minnesota, Indigenous children are sixteen times more likely to experience out-of-home placements than are white children.[5]

Black, Indigenous, and brown parents do not mistreat their children at higher rates than white parents do.[6] Narratives about "bad parents" are as false and as anti-Black as narratives about "violent criminals" in prisons. Just as the language of criminal charges like "lewd conduct" or "assault" offers little accurate information about what actually happened, allegations and convictions of child neglect and child abuse are similarly unhelpful, inaccurate, and demonizing.

Mirroring what unfolds in other processes of policing and criminalization, the family policing system, at every stage, targets marginalized families and subjects them to more punitive surveillance. Federal data shows police are the most prevalent reporters of child abuse and neglect, driving the family policing system.[7] In addition, families from these communities are more likely to come into contact with individuals or institutions who will report them to child protective services and therefore are more likely to be investigated. These investigations tip families into a relationship with carceral systems. In some states, even being the subject of an unfounded allegation for child neglect places a person on a registry that can be used to deny employment or benefits.

Horrific statistics such as these—which, we should stress, are uncontested by state agencies—are not novel.[8] State systems of child welfare and protection—even those with decades-long public commitments to equity, cultural competence working groups, or required trainings for implicit bias—are unable to reduce the targeting of Black and Indigenous families. Yet our goal should not be ending racial disproportionality or ensuring that white or Asian American families, for example, experience the same rate of investigations or child removals as Black, brown, or Indigenous families. Rather our vision should start from the position that no kinship network benefits from investigations, surveillance, policing, or forced separation.

Child welfare and protection systems have never made children's lives—or the lives of the adults around them—safer or more secure. Far from ideal outcomes, involvement with the family policing system is violent: Young people in the foster care system have some of the worst life outcomes. Multiple reports, statements, blue-ribbon commissions, task force findings, and academic studies (most often propelled by Black feminists) highlight the failure of the child welfare system to protect young people.[9] Many communities are intimately aware that child welfare systems have never supported their children, kinship arrangements, or people. With deep roots in state-sanctioned racial and gender violence—for example, the state's multigenerational theft of Indigenous children through residential boarding schools and other forms of forced removal from families and lands—these systems are key perpetrators of racial, gender, sexual, and economic violence.[10]

Rather than the misleading language of child welfare or child protective services, activists directly impacted by the system as well as scholars such as Brianna Harvey, Victoria Copeland, and Dorothy Roberts, among many others, use the term *family policing* to squarely name the fact that these institutions and practices are far from benign or neutral. Predicated on an economy of hyper-individualization that strives to evade any trace of culpability or blame, these public and private institutions and bureaucracies also routinely deepen and reproduce vulnerabilities. Instead of the state's failure to regulate unfettered punitive carceral capitalism, to protect workers' rights, or to use public wealth to support public welfare, the individual caregiver is singled out as neglectful or abusive for failing to pick up their child on time from school, failing to clothe their child in appropriate winter clothing, failing to do laundry, or failing to secure adequate childcare. The state or employer is never indicted for failing to pay a living wage, while mothers and grandmothers are deemed criminally negligent and savagely attacked for filing false addresses in order to ensure their young people are enrolled in a school system they perceived as safer and better resourced. As these chapters document, the family policing system (FPS) is a core plank of the US carceral state.

The surveillance and policing of families is not cheap. Public dollars are always available to investigate and monitor marginalized folks—particularly Black mothers—while pennies are made available for direct support for families in need. One of the largest federal spending entitlement programs for children is the foster system, not social assistance or services that would go directly to kinship networks in need. Foster care funding represents 65 percent of federal funds dedicated to child welfare, and adoption assistance makes up another 22 percent. Funding sources that may be used for preventive and reunification services represent only 11 percent of the resources allocated to the federal child welfare program.[11] Politicians enact and strengthen punitive, increasingly public registries to surveil mothers who are reported for abuse.[12] Every state has some type of punitive registry to track both allegations *and* convictions of child maltreatment.[13]

The stakes are always high in our movements to end the prison industrial complex and to build the stronger and safer communities we need; the contexts that surround our work continue to shift. Across the globe, campaigns centering abolitionist demands have gained some traction and have resulted in some cultural shifts—for example, an increased scrutiny around policing budgets—but these temporary wins, which always ignite predictable and potent backlash, are not the finish line. And, as importantly, how we struggle matters! As we write this book's introduction, our demands to end the FPS in the US live in a landscape populated by other movements who demand parental rights and purport to protect children. Libertarians, Republicans, right-wingers, MAGA folks, and more agitate for parental rights to shut down access to all kinds of resources and possibilities for many, particularly young people, including gender-affirming medical care, abortion and other reproductive services, and access to basic sexual health information. The myth of parental choice—adroitly masking white supremacy, the naturalized inequities baked in capitalism, and transphobia—justifies the erosion and privatization of public systems like education and circulates throughout the contemporary wave of book bans, which reached historic numbers in 2024 according to the American Library Association.[14] At the end of 2024, these movements and demands coalesced with the MAGA electoral win.

While on the surface our language, and even some of our campaigns, might overlap with these demands for parental rights, fundamental and foundational political differences exist between our organizing to end the FPS and the 2024 wave of right-wing appeals to parental rights. We assert that the FPS flourishes because of foundationally toxic ideologies—heteropatriarchy, capitalism, colonialism, ableism, and white supremacy—and our work aims to dismantle these interlocking forms of oppression. Unlike racist and anti-feminist groups such as Moms for Liberty, we argue that these interlocking and oppressive ideologies both fuel the FPS and simultaneously represent who is often most targeted and criminalized. We also recognize that adultism, or the belief that young people and children are less than, has diminished all our lives. Capitalism—the economic system we live under—far from producing flourishing life pathways for all, uses myths such as "parental choice" as a distraction, while the wealthy continue their tax strike, hoarding resources and opportunities. Organizing against the FPS continues to name and challenge these deeply harmful economic and belief systems, which the current whitestream parental rights movement actively reinforces and valorizes.

The organizing represented throughout this book is again too urgent. The 2025 federal administration has explicitly promised aggressive crackdowns on migrants, abortion access, and transgender lives. In our efforts to resist this targeting and support our communities, we must not overlook how these bodies are interconnected and intimately tied to many other lives and pressing challenges. For example, families are separated not only by nation-state borders but also by the wider prison industrial complex, which incarcerates and separates loved ones—particularly women, mothers, sisters, and caregivers—in ways that are often rendered less visible in mainstream discourse. As we fight for migrant rights and against the violence of borders, let us not deploy arguments or tactics that actively harm other communities. Can our work to protect those targeted for mass deportation also amplify the struggles and needs of those isolated by incarceration or those punished by the family policing systems, who are also forcibly separated from loved ones? The ongoing struggle for bodily autonomy, especially for gender-nonconforming and transgender youth, also highlights how queer and transgender adult caregivers are being criminalized and framed as threats to all young people. The narrow whitestream frame of reproductive justice—often reduced to abortion rights—must again be expanded to encompass the broader, equally urgent right to parent, care for, and remain connected to our families—however we define this kinship network. Reproductive justice is about abortion rights but is also fundamentally about the right to care, to protect, and to be in community with those we love.

We are not asking any one individual to carry every fight at once; this is neither possible nor effective. As the state pits vulnerable communities against each other and strives to define our "issues" and to police our languages and histories, we must resist. We need collective and integrated strategies and a commitment to the belief that no one is disposable. Our campaigns, which aim to work against facets of this regime, must be open and coalitional and not pivot on any particular group's exceptionality. In our reactive mode—for example, when we challenge harmful policies and offer direct support and mutual aid for those targeted—can we also think and act widely and preventively, beyond the confines of this specific campaign or project? Of course this is not easy, and we won't all agree. Coalition spaces, a fertile site for principled struggle, should not be comfortable spaces, as organizer and musician Bernice Johnson Reagon reminded feminists in 1981.[15] One of our movement's strengths is precisely that these forms of state violence are intertwined and we can build solidarity and coalitions, and by doing so we can experiment with our own grammar for freedom and liberation.

To build a world beyond policing, we name and challenge the carceral or punitive logics at the core of most state services or institutions, particularly those that profess to be caring or supportive. Our vision does not oppress or subordinate the child, does not construct caretaker and child as adversarial or oppositional, and highlights that caretaking is complex, relational, and risky. Rejecting rigid formations of family, we explore kinship networks in their most expansive and flexible forms: as community, as queer. Unearthed from the hands of Black, Indigenous, and brown mamas, our forms of care, kinship, and family are antithetical to the white-supremacist desire for power and control over young bodies. Contributors to this project dare to believe that we can take care of each other, listen to both parents and children, and embrace the tension and the alignment of generational relationships.

◆

We came together because of our overlapping experiences and values, propelled by our political moment. Our years of intersecting and collective feminist organizing consistently remind us that the FPS is deprioritized and erased, even as abolitionist campaigns mature. Despite these setbacks, we know that people have been organizing against the FPS for generations without any fanfare and often with significant and harmful consequences. Chapters aim to center the analysis and experience of those unsung people, often those directly harmed by these systems, and our networks who continue to work collectively to resist and experiment and build other pathways for safety, healing, and community..

While the stories and examples in this book hold some answers, we offer only a snapshot of the many opportunities for engagement and transformation; there are activists, organizers, and actions that we were unable to include, and we hope this book can lead readers toward those other radical possibilities. Our call to ourselves and for readers is to continue to imagine ways of living beyond policing: Build and practice experiments that grow safety. Stay with the messiness, together.

While we are beyond outraged and heartbroken, we are also organized.

OUTRAGE

1

It's Never Been About
the Welfare of Children
The Origins of the Term *Family Police*

Brianna Harvey and Jasmine Wali

*Challenging family policing has and always will be
rooted in community. In this spirit, our contribution is a
conversation where we reflect on and discuss the collective
evolution of the terms used to describe the system that
fails to protect but has immense capacity to police.*

Jasmine Wali: Thanks, Brianna, for having this conversation with
me today as we reflect back on the language we use to describe a system many call the "child welfare system." For so long, I have known
that this system does not promote child welfare, but it wasn't until I
read "Surveillance of Black Families in the Family Policing System"

by Victoria Copeland and Maya Pendleton that I heard that term used to describe this system.[1] Can you talk a bit more about how you got to that idea?

Brianna Harvey: The idea of family policing isn't a recent development. Historically, Black and brown communities have always perceived social workers and the foster system as another form of law enforcement that surveilled, criminalized, and investigated their families. Victoria and I discussed this a lot and were determined to amplify a powerful, deeply felt experience that has been shared and discussed by impacted folks and in organizing spaces for years. While many other academics had explained how this system failed to deliver "care," "welfare," or "protection" for Black and Indigenous families for decades, we were really looking to find a way to de-sanitize the system from the outset.[2] We wanted to transfer the intellectualism of communities into the academic and movement discourse, and this required us to rethink every term and framework we were using to describe this violent system.

Previously many scholars flagged that the child welfare system "policed" bodies, and while this is true, this framing felt insufficient. Policing is one way the system acts, rather than pointing to the way the system is designed. We learned from abolitionists fighting prisons and jails that the logic of policing extends way beyond a particular act, and we felt that redefining this system as the "family policing system" would immediately identify the function and purpose of this system.[3]

Using the "family policing system" would allow us to connect the work to broader struggles against the prison industrial complex (PIC), which for years have fought to bring attention to the ways that systems of surveillance, control, and punishment extend beyond the criminal legal system to impact families, communities, and marginalized groups.[4] This felt significant to us, and many others. By shifting the way we spoke about this system, we were building movement solidarity and could grapple with frameworks developed by PIC abolitionist groups like Critical Resistance in a meaningful way, and we could encourage our comrades in PIC spaces to build more intersectional analyses.

JW: The term resonates with people because it captures the punitive nature of a system that has similar practices to the police. For example, in a typical police investigation, officers can search your car, your home, and your body. Caseworkers have the same authority. They can search your home, look through your cabinets and drawers, see what kind of food is in your home, strip-search your kids, question your kids, your neighbors, and family—and then make their judgment calls.[5] They have the power to separate your family. And just like with police, the majority of people targeted and impacted by this system are Black, Indigenous, and low-income.[6]

BH: Building on what you said, there are a lot of ways that caseworkers for this system exert control over families similar to police. Rarely when social workers knock on the door of a family's home do they have a warrant, yet most families feel like they have to let them into their home and permit an investigation, because families don't want to lose their children and don't want to appear uncooperative or suspicious. Unfortunately the minute the door opens, people are opening up their families to harm. The system also imparts this "personal responsibility" narrative against parents without taking into account how families are victimized by larger systems. Families are punished and labeled neglectful for their inability to meet their families' basic needs, even while residing in under-resourced communities facing poverty, violence, and systemic racism. Rather than being seen as resilient or resourceful, families are blamed for the challenging conditions they endure. Instead of helping families achieve stability, the system removes children from their parents and tears apart families.

JW: And an investigation is just one facet of an entire ecosystem of tools used to monitor families. For example, I'm thinking of the practice of mandated reporting laws, which require people in certain helping professions to report any "suspicion" of child abuse or neglect. This includes people who work in hospitals, clinics, schools, shelters, and other institutions that provide "helping" services.[7] This means that when people are seeking help, they find themselves under the eye of the system without their knowledge. Employees are deputized to report suspicions—and are taught that it's better to report than not, and that they can face employment or legal consequences if they don't make the call. So, where can families go for help?

BH: Like you mentioned, mandated reporting is really a gateway into the system. Myself and other scholars have talked about this concept of "multi-system collusion," which describes how systems collude or work together and harm people of color through their practices and policies.[8] For example, schools collude with the family policing system by being the number one entity that reports families, in particular Black families, for suspected maltreatment. Interestingly, the quality of reports from school personnel is actually pretty poor and usually unfounded. School personnel, including teachers and administrators, believe the false narrative that this system is here to help families and connect them to resources. School personnel often contact the child abuse hotline expecting to receive support for their students, but instead, families end up entangled in a system that ultimately leaves them in a worse situation. Also, it's no accident that historically the families who receive the most reports and investigations from the family policing system are located in the poorest communities that have the highest police presence.

JW: Definitely. And it's so important to understand the history to know how we got here, right? Because the "child welfare" system has always been a system for poor families. Foster "care" started from orphan trains in the mid-1800s. White children were shipped from New York City to foster homes in the Midwest, but the majority weren't actually orphans.[9] They were just poor. Indigenous children were taken from their homes and put in boarding schools under the guise of "child welfare."[10] Black families have long been separated, from slavery through the Jim Crow era, until now.[11] Each iteration of abolishment of various forms of systemic oppression led to another system. Abolishing slavery led to Jim Crow.[12] And one by-product of abolishing overt Jim Crow policies was this new system that polices families. Let me explain. Amid the civil rights movement, activists and poverty lawyers helped Black families get the welfare benefits they were entitled to but had long been blocked access to by state and federal policy and system actors.[13] In the early 1960s, only about one-third of eligible families were enrolled for welfare benefits; by 1971, about 90 percent received benefits—causing welfare costs to skyrocket.[14] In order to portray Black families as undeserving of these welfare benefits, the (white) public blamed impoverished Black parents for being poor and critiqued Black parenting.[15]

Backlash to the gains of the civil rights movement fueled hyper-visible anti-Black rhetoric that centered on parenting. And this time period set the foundation for the 1974 Child Abuse Prevention and Treatment Act (CAPTA), which federally codified poverty as child neglect and shifted away from antipoverty measures and towards blaming parents for poverty.[16] There's a through line from the history of this system focused on the moral failings of people experiencing poverty and anti-Black and anti-Indigenous racism. When I hear "family policing," I also think of the welfare and social workers who conducted "man in the house" searches on Black families receiving welfare, showing up at odd times to check if a man was home, and then welfare benefits could be removed—literally policing the family.[17] These same surprise visit tactics are used by caseworkers today.

BH: The system's history and the continued expansion of CAPTA just reinforce that this is not a benevolent system. This is a system that is amassing billions of dollars and is in the business of destroying families.[18] A lot of money is in circulation, and people benefit from the system staying the way it is. I think that's why so many people fight against the abolition of the family policing system. It has nothing to do with concern over child safety.

The notion that less system involvement with families or its absence would lead to more child abuse and child deaths is a false narrative. At the beginning of the Covid-19 pandemic, the number of child abuse reports and investigations significantly decreased, because kids weren't in school and school personnel weren't surveilling and reporting young people. Instead, children were at home with their family members. There was no increase in child deaths or substantiated maltreatment, debunking this idea that we need this system to surveille and police families for "child safety."[19]

JW: I want to expand more on the idea of policing and how it shows up for all of us. I was talking with a parent whose kids' school had installed laundry machines in the basement to help families, since there were so many children coming to school without access to washing machines. The school was helping kids wash their clothes, but they were still reporting kids for coming to school with dirty clothes. Even in schools that have recognized an issue and created solutions to assist families, they are still not exempt from the strong sense of individualism that is rooted in this country's foundation and codified in policies like CAPTA. This reminded me of organizations I've worked with that speak to the importance of mutual aid—yet even in their own mutual aid projects, they police how people spend funds, criticize people if they ask for more, and even block folks from accessing future support if they aren't showing up in the "right" ways. Even if a school or organization has the resource, they can be critical of parents for not using it in the way or the time they want to.

The idea that poverty is a moral failing is so ingrained in all of us. We're inundated with messages that it's shameful to ask for financial help, because those who struggle financially have some supposed moral defect. And in the same vein, we are taught that it is humiliating to be financially taken advantage of. We see this reflected in anti-Black rhetoric around welfare in the '60s and '70s—the false narrative that Black women were having babies to take advantage of the welfare system was used to fuel a politicized rage from the (white) public.

And I see this fear of being financially "taken advantage of" in myself, in my community, in organizations and schools, and in the government. It's the cop inside our own head. And what this means for our work with families is that we start to believe that we can only help a family so much, or for so long, before we are being taken advantage of—or that at some point, a parent must figure things out on their own, and if they can't, they are a bad parent. This, too, is a form of policing. And I think this type of policing mindset is broader than what I just mentioned and exists across race and class lines. So my question to you, Bri, is: Why won't simply increasing diversity among caseworkers, social workers, and judges impact the system?

BH: I fully agree: Diversity will not save the system. As a Black woman, and someone who worked as a social worker for over twelve years, I think back to my own motives when I entered the profession. I wanted to be a social worker so that I could help families. And I think a lot of social workers enter the profession with this same mindset, especially people from marginalized backgrounds, including people who are former foster youth. But the problem is that this system is set up in such a way that the work of individual social workers won't throw it off course or make it deviate from its practices. The system is still going to do exactly what it was created to do. Therefore, even if there are more Black and brown caseworkers, these social workers of color are put in positions where they have to uphold the values and the practices of the system and are the policing agents causing harm to the communities they initially wanted to protect. Jasmine, you have done a lot of work with the community, and I'm curious what impact you have seen the system have on families?

JW: As a social worker, I've seen family separation be deeply traumatizing to both children and parents.[20] The majority of people who have been separated from their family seek out their family and want to build or rebuild relationships. How many have done a 23andMe genetic test? Many people want to connect with their family and ancestry, and forced separation takes that away from children. It's traumatizing to a child to be torn from their family, to not understand why they were taken away from everything they know and love, and to not know why their parents couldn't protect them from whatever was to come in the foster placement. Once a child is in the system, their responses to this trauma are criminalized. Foster caregivers and group homes call the police on kids for "acting out."[21] Many are put on psychotropic medication at young ages to "control" their behavior.[22]

Parents are traumatized too. The system dehumanizes parents through court appearances, supervised visits, and "services" that are designed to critique one of the most personal practices: parenting. It's traumatizing to a parent to tear their children away and to feel like they weren't able to protect their children from the system.

Rebuilding family relationships after forced separation is beyond difficult, and families are rarely given resources to heal.

Consider what kids must feel towards their parent: Why didn't you protect me? Why did you allow them to take me away? Did you fight for me? And consider what parents must feel: My kid doesn't respect me anymore. My kid may never forgive me. The feelings of anger, guilt, and shame reverberate.

BH: I think you are bringing up really important points about the impact on families. It makes me think about the work of historian Peggy Cooper Davis, who writes about slavery, the law, and Black families. She writes about how the institution of slavery perpetuated this idea of "parental helplessness," where parents didn't have any autonomy over the lives of themselves or their children due to being enslaved.[23] Instead they experienced forced separation, and the imposed dissolution of their families at the hands of their enslaver. I feel like that's exactly what this system does to Black families. It takes away parents' rights and ability to make decisions for their lives, and forcibly separates them from their children. So, where do you think we go from here, Jasmine?

JW: I think we have to know the history of this system and how it carries on the legacy of anti-Black and anti-Indigenous racism that's foundational to this country—because that legacy seeps into our own beliefs and practices. Families need unconditional support, they need antipoverty programs like cash assistance, a higher minimum wage, health care, childcare, and so on.[24] All of these initiatives have been shown to decrease reports of child abuse and neglect. But the way that the system is set up—with constant barriers to getting help in order to decrease "dependency" on the system—actually creates the conditions for a report to the system. The idea that we can only help a family so much before they become "dependent," so we make our processes to get welfare or shelter or health care so convoluted that it's actually more challenging to raise a family: This creates the conditions for a report. We have to look in ourselves and check our anti-Black biases and the cop inside our own head, and apply this on a broader scale and advocate for unconditional antipoverty support for families.

BH: I agree with everything you said, and I think we have to spend more time listening to the youth and impacted folks that have been trapped in this system if we want to move forward. Throughout my career, the youth I have worked with have always been adamant that they wished their families weren't criminalized for being poor. None of them ever shared that they were thankful to have been removed from their homes. They just wished their families could have received the support and access to resources that they needed to have a stable home environment. Like you mentioned, we need to demand unconditional support and focus on investing in communities and meeting the needs of those that systems target and exploit. We have to move away from this personal accountability narrative against parents and take a critical look at the role of systemic oppression and how it continues to perpetuate the challenges faced by families. Meeting the needs of families and abolishing harmful systems should be the primary focus.

2

Who Is Safe? Who Is Protected?

Corey B. Best

Who is safe? Who is protected? Over a decade ago, my response to these questions would have been based on the belief that safety entails placing vulnerable children outside their natural environment and far removed from their parents and families. I am quite unnerved and embarrassed to acknowledge that in 2010 I was conditioned to act as a contorted minstrel of myself. In many ways, I assimilated and accepted the invitation into whiteness. In accepting this invitation, the cuts, wounds, and toxicity within "systems change" meetings in my work as a community organizer left me aching, shrinking, and immobilized, while deepening my loss of self-determination and sense of isolation. I realized after a year of these work meetings that no one is safe if safety is defined by systems of oppression that judge, punish, and sentence families, specifically Black, brown, and impoverished folks, to a life of torment.

Perhaps like many readers of this book, I learned that disadvantaged experiences provide pathways for an advantaged analysis.

Before being able to confidently accept the invitation to move to outrageous action as a freedom seeker, I had blind spots, deferred dreams, inferiority complexes, and gaping holes in my soul from years of racist beatdowns and being marked as a criminal.

Important note: I entered the culture of white-dominant arenas six years after experiencing the civil death penalty, which is also known as "termination of parental rights." This is where my political consciousness around the family policing system emerged. (More will be revealed later in this chapter, so keep reading.) My physical parental bond was forcibly severed while I was being held in a cage in a New Orleans jail. In the presence of the white gaze, expressing feelings of being unsafe was off limits for me. I knew from the very first "family involvement" meeting that safety for me was having diapers, a job, enough to pay Amscot back for that payday loan, and a few people to talk mad smack with when I was bored. I quickly grew to understand that family policing and state actors across institutions were not saviors. They were executioners. Safety was an illusion. I took several ass whoopings in those harsh containers while challenging their definition of safety and before remembering in my soul who I belonged to. And who I belong to has *always* allowed me to be brave enough to feel a sense of safety.

I was reared and built in Chocolate City. Safety was a vibe that was felt through communal experiences in my family and with my friends. Safety lived within my neighborhood on G Street in Washington, DC. The year 1995 was a pivotal moment for me to shapeshift beyond the false category of "super predator." My closest friends and I—the comrades that become cousins and brothers—embarked on a journey to atone, reconcile, and take responsibility for dreaming and actualizing a world that had not been imagined yet—a world without cages.

On that October day in 1995, the Million Man March in Washington, DC, anchored my beliefs in my Blackness and solidified my hopes of becoming more than a corner boy. This action pushed me to reckon with ways of being *big* in a cage that was designed to keep my people believing we needed an imperialistic government to do for us what we historically have always been able to do for ourselves. Outside of books and TV, the march was my introduction to what the rhythm of fearless movement felt like in my body. On the walk, we were on hyperalert because of the vast police presence and from the everyday policing that is real for Black bodies, including the looks from white bodies who were at the time scattered in selective DC neighborhoods. Silent police bodies were on full alert waiting for racial trauma to erupt through hundreds of Black boys and men who were traveling to the National Mall to be consumed with invigorating musings, stories, history, and the artistry of Louis Farrakhan, Reverend Jeremiah Wright, Rosa Parks, and Maya Angelou.

As a Black man, my Black mama and grandmother always provided safety, regardless of the struggle du jour. Therefore, I learned to value how my Black manhood is seen through the eyes, hearts, and souls of Black women. Maya Angelou hit me the hardest as she delivered her Million Man March poem. I was uplifted, as if she reached into my core and held my heart up to her eyes. Angelou's words literally shaped parts of my becoming a freedom fighter:

> The hells we have lived through and live through still,
> Have sharpened our senses and toughened our will.
>
> . . . .

The ancestors remind us, despite the history of pain
We are a going-on people who will rise again.[1]

In this 400,000-person sea of dreamers, organizers, teachers, and healers, I felt enveloped in physical, emotional, and psychological bravery. I wanted more! This experience drifts in and out of my standing memory. I was only a twenty-two-year-old man who had not yet developed a deepened political analysis. Nor did I possess the chops to embrace freedom as the love story that evokes empathy and spurs an individual and collective struggle for a world without cages. There have been many moments since that day in 1995 that I have fallen back into the miseducation provided by those white-dominant institutions to which I ascribed power at the time.

I went to the march because I believed I was attached to a collective struggle. I believed I would notice and hold safety with other men who had experienced imperial occupation, brutality, random searches, countless stops, and perpetual harassment at the hands of the cops. Three years following the march, I was introduced to Kwame Ture and Charles V. Hamilton's 1967 book *Black Power: The Politics of Liberation*.[2] I was mesmerized by the authors' courage and bravery during constant whitelash and resistance. This book taught me that Black bodies were told to endure life while the government hoarded the resources. The teachings of countless Black freedom fighters moved me to understand and embrace Black power as an invitation to move toward liberation and freedom, and away from reliance on systems that cause us perpetual harm.

I realized that what Black bodies were experiencing was by design. Black power threatens that design. Black power demands that we organize and expose the historical truth that our political, legal, social, and economics contracts with white society have never been honored. Safety is not something Black people experience, yet safety is a human right for all. Both things are true at once. Our society is steeped with carceral logic and a ferociously insatiable appetite for devouring Black bodies. Anti-Blackness showed up in me as my own fear to self-determine and speak against state violence. The denial of my worth was a denial of my people's collective value and power.

The context for Ture and Hamilton's book offers important historical teachings for today. In 1967, President Lyndon B. Johnson established what is now known as the Kerner Commission.[3] The commission was charged with uncovering the answers to three questions related to racial unrest and disturbance in the 1960s: (1) What happened? (2) Why did it happen? (3) What must be done to prevent it from happening again? Its goal was to better understand what led to and prompted "racial civil disorders" in 150 cities across the nation during the summer of 1967. The 1968 report highlights the white advantage gap and names white supremacy as the problem: "What white Americans have never fully understood but what the Negro can never forget—is that white society is deeply implicated in the ghetto. White institutions created it, white institutions maintain it, and white society condones it."

This four-hundred-plus-page document identifies twelve grievances that have their origins in enslavement, including police practices, white attitudes, discriminatory consumer credit practices, and inadequate welfare programs. The report's final recommendations focus on three basic themes:

1. To mount programs on a scale equal to the dimension of the problems.

2. To aim these programs for high impact in the immediate future in order to close the gap between promise and performance.
3. To undertake new initiatives and experiments that can change the system of failure and frustration that now dominates the ghetto and weakens our society.

You might already be asking yourself: What happened? Why have I never heard of this report?

The report was buried, never addressed during any State of the Union. This report names the problems correctly: Racism is the cause of unsafe community conditions. Our Blackness is not the problem. The report also teaches me that the past holds valuable lessons that abolitionists can draw on to complete the love story of freedom.[4]

One key learning for me is that our relationships with family policing agents and other violent institutions must be reexamined and abandoned. We hold a collective capacity to use every human resource within our grasp to abolish all institutions sanctioned by the state to destroy our people. We are just about sixty years into civil rights legislation, and white bodies remain structurally and philosophically the only protected ones in this country. Advantages have shielded many, particularly white bodies, by systemically keeping them safe and free to make mistakes without oversurveillance, excessive force, social control, maximum sentences, and limited access to everyday social benefits.

For me, the questions of safety and protection require considerable thought and deliberation. As I journal daily, I come to the same conclusion—no one is safe and protected until we all are safe and protected. I must break my rigid attachments to government systems. I must work to realign my right relationships with people who share similar values and together create entry points for shared political commitment to movement ecosystems. We need to come together across struggles and honor that each of our fights have common imperialistic legacies: colonization, enslavement, land theft, universal Christianity, cis-heteropatriarchy, and ableism. These legacies are why safety and protection remain a dream for those who are non-white. After all, we all fall from the ledge of whiteness.

My discussion of safety and protection is not complete without unearthing the violent destruction of millions of families by policing, including family policing. Twenty years ago, while sitting in the Orleans Parish Prison, I met the Adoption and Safe Families Act (ASFA) up close. This federal law was set in motion in 1997 by the Clinton administration, when crack was penetrating Black and brown communities across the country.

A few years before the birth of ASFA, the federal crime bill of 1994 gave the stamp of approval for states to pass even more tough-on-crime laws. By 1994, all states had passed at least one mandatory minimum law, but the crime bill encouraged even more punitive laws and harsher practices that resulted in locking up more bodies and for longer periods of time. Under the leadership of Bill Clinton, Democrats wanted to wrest control of crime as a political issue from Republicans, so the two parties began a bidding war to increase penalties for crime, trying to outdo one another. The 1994 crime bill was a key part of the Democratic strategy to be tougher on crime than Republicans. In this vein, the Personal Responsibility and Work Opportunity Reconciliation Act of 1996 was signed by Clinton, replacing the Aid to Families with Dependent Children program with the Temporary

Assistance for Needy Families program. This law fulfilled Clinton's campaign promise to "end welfare as we know it."[5]

By the time 2004 hit, ASFA was only seven years old. If we believed Clinton and policymakers, ASFA would free unsafe children up for adoption and set the stage for permanent living arrangements, largely outside a child's culture, community, and/or family. But there is nothing new about hiding an agenda that oppresses Black, brown, and impoverished families behind myths about safety. ASFA required states to begin initiating the process to terminate parental rights after "reasonable efforts" to reunify the child with their family. If "reasonable efforts" had been made and a child was controlled by the state and had been in foster care fifteen out of the last twenty-two months, the state was authorized to proceed with termination and to extract a child from their sacred familial roots.

A timeline of events of my own family paints a picture of what millions of families have gone through since 1997:

- On January 3, 2004, a report was made through the Louisiana child abuse hotline because two parents were yelling at each other.
- On January 4, 2004, two police officers entered my home and physically abused me with my two-year-old son sleeping ten feet away. I was arrested for domestic disturbance. Ten minutes after being placed in the squad car, an officer came down and placed my two-year-old in the front seat of the same squad car with a cop. They took my son to the family police, and I was booked into jail.
- On January 6, 2004, I was released from jail. I had my first meeting with a family police investigator.

- In February 2004, I was given only twice-weekly visits with my son by the family policing system.
- In April 2004, I was rearrested on a warrant and incarcerated in Orleans Parish Prison.
- On December 10, 2004, I faced a family policing judge at a termination of parental rights hearing while incarcerated and wearing orange, and she terminated my rights within twenty minutes of the start of the hearing.

From the day my child was removed to the day my rights were terminated: eleven months and six days. *Eleven months and six days.* In only twenty minutes, my son lost his right to his father. Families call ASFA the "civil death penalty." That is what I felt. For those who have never had this experience, it's like surviving a lethal injection.

Black families will experience safety only when the family policing institution has been dismantled. Today, I practice and aspire to remain in critical resistance against state violence. I have heard that abolition is practical if the values of commitment, right relationship, presence, truth, and collectivism are nurtured. My hope is that this essay, a love letter that is filled with stones, can knock sense into those who refuse to see that they, too, are dealing with internal displacement.

I invite readers back to yourself. To love yourself. Think of the injustice you were born to interrupt. I ask you to fully comprehend where you stand in relation to that injustice. As a future ancestor, what do people need to know about this injustice? Perhaps I am an unlikely witness, but I invite you to shift and awaken your consciousness and to build solidarity and empathy—and, yes, this might ignite a principled struggle in your core.

3

Prevention, Reparations, and Reunification
Black Families and Healing the Harms of Family Policing

jaboa lake

For my mother, Tanisha Sakala Jones; her children,
my sisters Jetta Starr, Jeannie Kelly, Jaycee Dakota,
and (Linda Rose); and for my siblings Niki Tylee
(HyeKung), Evelyn Mae, Montrell, Taylor, and TJ

For years my sisters and I kept track of our mother from limited, out-dated arrest records. Last year—ten months too late—I learned my mother passed away. Five minutes later, I learned that my grandmother, who we had been told had died twenty-five years ago, was alive. In a seven-minute phone call I lost a mother and gained a grandmother.

Between the ages of fourteen and fifteen, my mother, Tanisha, lost her father, was introduced to heroin, and became pregnant by a man nine years her senior. By the time she was twenty-two years old, she had four children—me and my sisters. In those years she was handling grief, addiction, pregnancies, assault, homelessness. Shortly after the youngest was born, my sisters and I were removed by the state and placed into foster homes. I was four or five years old the last time I saw my mother. In the state's eyes, she made bad choices, didn't care for us. But she, as a Black child with babies, was criminalized for the choices she made to care for us. What are choices when you have few or no options? "She wasn't protected," said my auntie Emma "Babydoll." "This should have never happened."

Over the next few years, my three sisters and I would be separated, placed into multiple foster homes, and adopted through a predominantly white Christian nonprofit agency that partnered with the state. My eight siblings, who are my everything, are Black, Tongan, Korean—my adoptive mother once said she "wanted one of every color." We all hold our own deep histories and stories, but adoption was seen as a solution for all of us. "Taking kids away and giving them a 'new family' should never be the solution," my sister Jeannie reflected. "And family isn't just parents. They took us away from all of that—grandparents, aunts, uncles, cousins. And [they took away] community, to be raised with people like us. I started thinking, who is this beneficial for? Why is that considered better?" We didn't see our family for twenty-five years.

The racist legacies and motivations of family separation

The family policing, child "welfare," and foster systems are traced back to control of Black bodies, Black women's bodies in particular, during enslavement; displacement of Native children to residential

schools and white settler families in the service of cultural genocide; and separation of migrant children and placement in the
foster system to enforce borders.[1] The family policing and foster
systems do not protect children, because at their formation, they
were never meant to. They were built and continue to uphold capitalist, colonial, and imperial power.[2] The family policing and child
welfare systems surveil and target Black mothers, while praising
white adoptive parents and providing financial incentives for adoption for potential parents through credits and subsidies, and for
agencies through state and federal grants.[3]

The racist legacies of family policing and separation manifest
in as many unique ways as families who have been impacted. The
state relies on false narratives, such as the "welfare queen," to uphold racially targeted policies and practices that actively disrupt
families and remove resources, while overlooking abuse by white
parents.[4] In our case, instead of receiving care, our mother was in
and out of incarceration her entire life, while our white adoptive
father, who sexually abused children for decades, has never had to
answer to a court.

Family separation is necessary to provide lives that uphold the
foster care–to–prison and the foster care–to–homelessness pipe-
lines, both of which provide billions of dollars annually to private
companies and maintain social control of communities of color.[5]
This model of control and the interlocking systems that support
it create conditions for harm, blame, incarcerating poor families
of color, separating families, and using punitive actions to enact
control. This model is similar to enslavement because that is how
it was born. We have to continue to investigate who benefits from
these systems and who is harmed.

Multigenerational impacts

For my family, we often talk about how these harms could have been prevented. What could care have looked like? What was needed? For me and my sisters, the "solutions" that were implemented (at times more than once) included:

- Removal of children
- Arrest
- Incarceration, including in jail, prison, and the county mental health facility
- Placement into the foster system: rehoming, rehoming, rehoming
- Adoption
- Surveillance
- Court-ordered restriction and isolation from familial and community support
- Court-ordered treatment in inpatient programs
- Court-ordered treatment in outpatient programs

Each of these "solutions" exacerbated harm and severed family, some for weeks, some for decades, some, like my mother, for the remainder of their lifetimes.[6] Yet some would say we were better for it. We weren't with our parents, who were young, who used, who were poor, who struggled with mental health. Our adoptive parents were often praised for saving us, only to enact new traumas behind closed doors. They were our saviors, even though our adoptive father admitted that we were brought into the household to be abused. I was only six years old, just months after joining the family, the first time he called me sexy. Our adoptive mother later admitted that we were a "mistake" that she was manipulated to make.

Dorothy Roberts has demonstrated that the child welfare system is punitive and specifically targets poor families of color, and poor Black and Native American families in particular.[7] After being removed from our family and placed into the foster system, my sister Jetta was regularly punished. "[I was] being put down and told I was a bad kid because I reacted like a kid with the fear of being split apart from my sisters again," she shared. When Jetta became a mother herself, she experienced a mental health crisis after multiple traumatic incidents that led to the removal of her first son. Being separated from her son "felt the same way [as] when I went into foster care [myself]. I was confused when he was taken away, because he was taken care of." She said the pain of her child being removed and the lack of mental health care for her to work through her trauma led to addiction. The next few years Jetta spent time in and out of jail, living in city parks and in mandated addiction-recovery programs. She gave birth to two more beautiful children. Both additions to the family increased surveillance by the state. "I felt trapped," she said. "Nothing was there to help me, the services felt like a test. It makes you paranoid. Instead of being cared for you are tested and judged."

To Jetta, lack of care during these times looked like lack of medical care while incarcerated and pregnant, character witnesses not being included in her court cases, and judgment from social workers who were there to "take away, not support" her and her children. "Some people think, 'She's an addict, she can't be a good mom.' But even on my worst days I'm going to do it for them, especially with their mental health. I want to feel safe for them in the ways we didn't."

My littlest sister, Jaycee, who was a newborn when we were re-moved from our family, says she's always struggled with feelings of abandonment. When her own four children were removed from her care, she said it took her a long time to adjust to being away from them. "It took me years to sleep through the night." She didn't want them to feel she had abandoned them.

Like most of my siblings, Jaycee experienced repeated trau-mas from guardians who were supposed to care for her. After ex-periencing medical mistreatment during the births of her children, losing housing, living in motels with her children and partner, and moving to unsafe housing conditions, Jaycee also experienced a mental health crisis. Within a few hours, police entered her home, removed her children, and took her to an unknown location. "They told me I was on a mental health hold, but they didn't tell me where I was at. I kept asking one of the nurses where I was, and she said, 'If you don't want help, you can just leave.' But I couldn't leave." Jaycee had been taken to a county mental health facility on an involuntary hold. I had immediately taken a sixteen-hour bus ride to find her. Only when I arrived as a family member and ad-vocate did county staff respond to some of her questions. While in this facility, Jaycee was never directly seen by a doctor. She was, however, placed on forced medication based on staff reports. At first, they refused to tell either me or Jaycee what medications she was being forced to take, including her dosage, or the implications for custody of her children.

While we advocated and cared for Jaycee's immediate health and release, her children's father's family searched for the babies. "They take your kids and don't tell you where they are. Even a fam-ily that was trying to care for them couldn't track them down." She reflected on the similarities of what happened to us when we were children with family who had been searching for us. "With my kids, there wasn't anybody to advocate for me. Nobody explained anything to me."

After Jaycee's children were placed into the foster system, she almost got her kids back, but she didn't have the care they needed yet. "They wanted me to be in a mental health facility, but they didn't try to help me keep my home. So, I lost my home and I can't have my kids without a home. They didn't believe in me, that I could get back into the world." Over the next few years, Jaycee lived in parks, transitional housing, and friends' cars. Though family had space for her, she would need to move out of the county or state. Being far from her children was not an option. "I never missed a visitation. I grew up with abandonment issues, and wanted to make sure my kids didn't feel that way. Their dad was in and out of jail, so he couldn't make it, but I always did."

Where do we go from here?

What could have prevented harm? What could have happened instead when harm did occur? Where do we go from here?

Prevention

Preventive change can come in two forms: reformist reforms or abolitionist reforms.[8] Reformist reforms are changes that often serve as a patch to alleviate, but not fix, an isolated or temporary problem while reinforcing the status quo that only continues to perpetuate policing.[9] Some reformist reforms within family policing look like:

- State central or child protection registries, which bar family members from caring for children under the guise of protection[10]
- The Adoption and Safe Families Act, which prioritized swift adoptions over family reunification[11]
- Risk assessment analytics and algorithms[12]
- Court-mandated drug abuse treatment programs.

These reforms target people of color and increase state surveillance, adding barriers to family reunification by fast-tracking adoption, forcing compliance and pathologizing recovery programs, and strengthening the interlocking medical and prison industrial complexes.[13] Ultimately, these reformist reforms strengthen the carceral state and will create new problems, necessitate future reparations, and likely trigger another cycle of system-upholding so-called changes.

Abolitionist reforms are transformative, with the ultimate goal of structural change. If the justification for family separation is lack of housing, food, or health care that is then framed as "neglect," then prevention could look like supporting housing, food, health care, and other basic needs to lift families out of poverty.[14] If the justification for family separation is a parent's mental health, then prevention could look like increased access to voluntary mental health and supportive trauma care. If the justification for family separation is a parent's substance use, then prevention could look like decriminalizing substance use and substance use disorders, harm reduction, and voluntary treatment and recovery.[15] If we are truly committed to creating conditions that prevent family separation and eliminate family policing and surveillance, abolition of the systems that uphold them is necessary.[16]

Repair and reparations

Though prevention is key, the family policing system has produced and continues to produce harm. Reparations advocates have expanded the framework as necessary not just for enslavement but for systems that are evolutions of enforcement of slavery, like Jim Crow laws, redlining, mass incarceration, the war on drugs, and family policing and separation.[17] The Movement for Black Lives' framework for reparations affirms that these harms are interconnected, impacting the lives of Black people and our communities in ways that are deeply integrated into our everyday experience, across systems.[18] Reparations, then, cannot be limited to direct cash payments for people impacted by these systems, but must additionally include nonrepetition of harm by divesting from systems of white-supremacist capitalism, such as the prison industrial complex, and investing in systems of care, such as housing supports, universal basic income, and universal health care. Under this framework, repair for family separation is a meaningful form of reparations.[19]

Within family policing and separation as systems of the state, reparations require compensation and restitution by the same state.[20] Restitution is intended to restore the original situation. However, the harms of family separation often cannot be restored. We cannot regain the years lost with family. We cannot undo the abuse we endured under foster care and from our adoptive parents. But efforts to reunite and reconnect families can be reparative. For many Black children adopted transracially, restitution could mean repaired ties to ancestors, histories, and claims to reparations as descendants of enslaved people.

After reconnecting with our family twenty-five years after forcible separation, Jeannie reflected on what it felt like: "We grew up with an overwhelming feeling of not being wanted, not being enough, being unlovable. But when [we reconnected with family], it felt affirming because they made sure we knew we were wanted, we were loved. [After adoption] our names were changed, we moved across the country twice. The situation just made it impossible for them to find us."

My auntie Babydoll now tells us about the efforts she went through to provide support for our mother, for us, before the state removed us without contacting family. "Tanisha was fifteen. Had she had just a little more assistance . . . So much has happened to our people, why can't we get reparations for what happened to you girls? To our parents? To their parents? To get reparations, America would have to say they did something wrong and say they're sorry. But if you never say sorry, you never did anything wrong. It's a cycle. It's a cycle."

Reuniting and recovering

Through a complicated web of discovery, my sisters and I have reconnected with both sides of my mother's family. We've met more than one hundred family members, attended reunions, joined holiday gatherings and Sunday dinners, shared camping trips, gone to concerts and festivals together, and enjoyed late nights in backyards and dive bars. We've reintroduced ourselves to each other and made up for lost time. We're learning what it means to be a niece, a granddaughter, and a cousin in a family with a lot of love to share.

We learned about the searches our family undertook to try to find us. Our auntie and uncle filed paperwork at the court. Our grandmother showed up to court three times, but the state lied and said she didn't. We were lied to and told she died. Our social worker told the adoption agency that there was no family looking for us, that no family was alive to care for us.

We think about all of the close encounters that could have brought us back together sooner. When Jaycee was in transitional housing, I would walk her four children to a nearby park to play. We didn't know that our mother went to the same park (she had just moved back to the area from across the country) or that our grandmother lived *directly across the street*. We learned that we had mutual friends, went to the same pool halls, attended the same marches for Black Lives. We had always been so, so close.

If we had won the abolition of family policing, my sisters and I would not have faced some of our traumas, and perhaps we would not have needed to reconnect with our family. We may have been able to say goodbye to our mother while she was still here. We did not get to grow up with cousins. We did not get to be loved by grandparents. We did not get to be parented by our mother. We lost birthdays, holidays, sleepovers at aunties' houses, washdays with grandma, dancing with uncles at family reunions, playing games during summers with cousins. So we try to build that now, with what we have, with where we are.

4

Young People Deserve Community Care

zara raven

————

"Where did they put you when they took you away from home?" my ten-year-old asked as we traveled on an Amtrak train. We were on our way to New Jersey, where I lived at thirteen when caseworkers removed me from my mother's care. My child's question is an insightful one—and is not asked often enough by proponents of family policing. What happens to kids when they're separated from their families? Are they put in jail? In psychiatric institutions? Sent to homes where they face physical or sexual abuse? Are they on the streets? Are they safe?

For those of us who experienced abuse both in our families of origin and in our foster homes, this is the most important question. While family reunification is now often identified by social service agencies as the ideal end goal, many social workers still argue for family separation in extreme cases of abuse. Yet terms like "extreme" and "abuse" are rarely defined, and what happens to kids after displacement from home receives little attention.

Mine is likely the kind of story some would say is an extreme case of abuse. My mother is a survivor of intimate partner abuse, born into a line of Caribbean women abused by their partners. She was raising two kids alone with limited resources when she met, and was charmed by, a man. They got engaged, and she became pregnant. This man emotionally abused my mother, and once she decided she wanted to leave, he reported her for child abuse. I was eight years old at the time, and it's hard to know, even now, if his claim was at all founded.

I remember being interviewed the first time by a caseworker in the one-bedroom apartment the five of us shared in New York City. I knew I didn't want to be taken away from my siblings, from my mother, from everything I knew. *And to where?* We said our mother didn't hit us. We stayed together.

Shortly after my brother was born, my mother left her fiancé and took us to New Jersey. She hung the US flag outside our door, signaling to the neighbors: *We're one of you.* But caseworkers from the Division of Youth and Family Services were already in our lives, and they showed up routinely and at random times.[1] Sometimes they came to check the cupboards to see if we had enough food. Sometimes they showed up at school, pulled me out of class, and took me through their questions.

I'm sure I ran through the same responses to their questions: "yes," "no," "sometimes," "not that much," "it's not that bad." Caseworkers didn't come bringing grocery bags, gas money, or money to keep the lights on and a roof over our heads. They didn't take a shift watching us while our mother worked. They came to rummage through the cupboards and keep an eye on the only Puerto Rican single mom on this suburban block, surveilling her every move to catch her when she slipped up.

And she did. She yelled, she hit us, she lost control. She sought to regain control, to prove that she could be the mother and the father and the worker, to uphold the American "family values" she'd learned from relying on assimilation as her primary survival strategy.

As a disabled queer light-brown-skinned child, my inability to conform cast me out of the family network. I was to be controlled and, if I couldn't be controlled, then thrown out or locked away.

The day the caseworkers took me from my mother's home, I'd been locked in the basement. A caseworker told me to pack a bag and get in the car. I didn't know where I was going or for how long. I hadn't seen or heard from my sister in days. I didn't know where she was. I didn't know until months later that they took my brother next.

None of us were asked about what we wanted to happen or what we needed to be safe. We were taken from each other, from our friends, from our schools, from everything we knew, with no plan, no preparation, and no support in the aftermath.

Over the next two years, I was shuffled around at least a half dozen times. I had my own room in a house on Long Island and in an apartment in Washington Heights. I slept on a sofa bed in an office in Spanish Harlem. No one was on the hook to take me to the doctor or dentist or to buy me a winter coat. No one asked, or listened, or supported me when I was assaulted in one of these homes.

Like many young people, I eventually left and took my safety into my own hands, surviving through some combination of trading sex for a place to sleep and asking strangers for money on the street.

For a long time, I believed my experience was an anomaly, a glitch in the matrix. I was sure the system worked out better for other kids, other families. And then I learned the data: About 50 percent of young people experiencing homelessness have experienced family policing.[2] Queer and trans young people are overrepresented in the system and on the street: 30 percent of youth in the family policing system and 40 percent of youth experiencing homelessness are lesbian, gay, bisexual, transgender, or queer (LGBTQ).[3] Most queer and trans homeless youth are Black and Latine.

Young people experience homelessness as they run from, or get put out of, homes where they experience physical or sexual abuse or rejection of their queer and trans identities. Queer and trans young people who experience rejection or abuse have limited options to access support or affirming resources outside their families of origin and their foster homes.

The violence inside the house

For Black, queer, trans, and disabled youth, the family policing system enacts the most severe violence, but they also experience harm caused by their family. The family, in its nuclear form, acts as a border that determines who is deserving of care and who gets excluded, shut out, or removed. Mirroring the borders around the nation-state, the border around a nuclear family is meant to weed out those who can't or won't conform to oppressive hierarchies structured by ableism, defined by Talila A. Lewis as "a system of assigning value to people's bodies and minds based on societally constructed ideas of normalcy, productivity, desirability, intelligence, excellence, and fitness. These constructed ideas are deeply rooted in eugenics, anti-Blackness, misogyny, colonialism, imperialism, and capitalism."[4] The border is reinforced by the popular myth of "stranger danger" or the idea that the real threat of violence exists outside the family or the nation-state.

Once again, the data paints a different picture. Intimate partner violence is a leading cause of violent death among women, with

Black women six times more likely to be killed by an intimate partner than their white counterparts.[5] More than 90 percent of youth survivors of sexual abuse were abused by a family member, caregiver, or someone close to them.[6]

Accurately portraying the realities of child abuse is challenging in part because there is no clear definition of abuse, because it is normalized, and because the people who perpetrate the harm are overwhelmingly known to children and are not strangers.

Although abuse is most often associated with physical violence, abuse is about power, not violence. Abuse is a system of maintaining power and control over someone, often exacerbated by existing power imbalances in our society, as in the power of adults over children. A power imbalance doesn't necessarily imply that abuse is always taking place. Abuse involves the use of controlling behaviors, such as belittling, intimidation, and physical violence, to uphold the power imbalance. In an adultist society, it is often viewed as normal when adults exhibit these behaviors against children.

Adultism, the systematic oppression of children and young people, is a form of ableism. Yolanda Williams from the network Parenting Decolonized writes that adultism devalues the body and minds of children.[7] In an adultist society, respect isn't defined by listening to and honoring the needs, boundaries, and experiences of others. Instead, respect is based on how well young people obey authority and conform to ableist norms. Children are objectified by messages like "kids are property to be seen and not heard." In this context, the abuse of children isn't the exception—it's the norm.

Yet when caregivers do contravene dominant norms, the state can and does punish these families. When the family fails to fulfill its function to uphold the ableist norms of the dominant culture, the state intervenes, asserting itself as "the central organizer of violence."[8] In Texas, for example, families that support and affirm the gender of their trans kids become targets of family separation policies, because support is equated with abuse.[9] In reinforcing the oppressive norms of the dominant culture, family policing increases violence against youth who are already most vulnerable.

In this system, disabled Black queer and trans youth were never meant to survive.[10]

Building communities of care

What if we challenged the systems and conditions that make children and young people unsafe, that make them vulnerable to violence in the first place? What if we continuously build and expand communities of care to ensure that children and young people have many places to turn to get their needs met?

The gap between our needs and our access to care remains wide, but we have many models from trans, queer, disabled, and sex-worker history. Queer and trans people of color have always built networks of care out of necessity, knowing we need each other to survive. In New York City in the 1970s, trans women-of-color organizers Marsha P. Johnson and Sylvia Rivera created Street Transvestite Action Revolutionaries (STAR) House for unhoused trans and queer youth of color, especially those trading sex to survive, to access peer support and safety while organizing for revolutionary change. Similarly, Young Women's Empowerment Project in Chicago was a radical collective for trans and cis young women and girls in the sex trades that published participatory action research about how to keep each other safe in the face of state and interpersonal violence.

Learning from our histories surfaces creative ways to survive and keep each other safe.

For two years I had the joy of coordinating Queenie's Crew, a program of Project NIA that engaged children in learning to build communities of care without prisons or policing. Each month, children took an action to bridge the gap across prison walls and to build the world that we need. Kids created pod maps, mapping out whom in their communities they can turn to if they cause or experience harm.[11] Kids practiced making zines to express their feelings and needs in conflict, and they played games to learn to spot the differences between an inaccessible, overpoliced community and the kind of community that can keep us safe. Kids researched the police budgets in their communities and created their own city budgets. Kids wrote Mother's Day cards to incarcerated mamas.

Queenie's Crew also supported caregivers to come together to talk about how we practice our values at home, ways we struggle, systems that make our lives more difficult, and how kids and caregivers often lack the support and resources needed to care for each other.

In Philadelphia, I work with others to rebuild and coordinate the childcare collective after a long pandemic-induced pause. The Philly Childcare Collective seeks to build intergenerational movements for collective liberation. Recognizing that caring for children is also a community responsibility, the Philly Childcare Collective is a powerful system for bringing people who aren't already parents into the fold as caregivers. Similar collectives exist in other places, including the Bay Area, Washington, DC, Detroit, and Portland.

Concept by zara raven. Art by Mar Erazo. Available in *Building Communities of Care: An Activity Book by Queenie's Crew* at queeniescrew.com.[12]

Most importantly, I practice this work at home, creating in my microcosm the interdependent way of life required for Black, disabled, queer, and trans survival. In my village, I am raising three Black and mixed-race, queer and trans, and disabled children with two other disabled queer loved ones. Each of us became solo parents in different ways—through death, separation, and choice. We came together through our commitments to youth liberation, disability justice, queer and trans liberation, Black liberation, and Mad pride. We came together through our commitments to each other and to care as a collective responsibility.

In our chosen family, we share care of our children, trading off weekends with the kids while maintaining close relationships with each other. We don't wait for conflict or harm to occur to talk about our relationships. We regularly hold restorative circles to proactively address our conflicts, express appreciation of each other, and invite the children to express their needs of each other and of us as their adults. Our circles have involved art, crafts, games, and poetry and have centered on safety planning, care mapping, and conflict transformation. We leave our circles with tangible action steps, making visible our needs and expectations of each other. We model for our kids the process of conflict and repair, and we engage them in the messy practice of living.

Our first time traveling together, we went to Puerto Rico, where four out of six of us have ancestral roots. We ate pastelitos and mofongo, danced bomba and salsa, and ran our fingers and toes through the ocean and sand. And we got on each other's nerves, and we fell apart and came back together. This kinship network is my village, and we recognize healing as an act of restoration and repair, as a continual act of returning to our own lineages and to the communal practices of care that allowed our queer and trans and disabled ancestors to survive.

We know we need each other, and we know we can count on each other. We've built a space where the adults are accountable to children, where all of us can play with gender and express big feelings. We can make mistakes. We can take breaks. We know that caring for those at the margins, especially Black disabled queer and trans folks, creates safety for everyone. We're building the model of intergenerational interdependence that we need, here and now.

This week, my daughter told me something that upset her involving others in our village. Before I could respond, she said, "I'm going to bring it to circle." We keep falling apart, and coming back together, and actively creating the care and conditions we need to be safer.

5

Abolish the Family

Ignacio G. Hutía Xeiti Rivera

Funny stories?

Have you been in a huddle with other adults and heard the "funny" stories about childhood experiences of backhands, beatdowns, or public humiliations?

At some gathering—whether at a dinner party or while reminiscing about our childhood with friends—the topic of disciplinary actions arises. From recounting the absurd and amusing antics of children, to seeking advice on teenage issues, these narratives of our upbringing shape our approach to parenting, our understanding of children, and our perception of power dynamics.

On another scale, these stories told in comic form serve as an opening. They surface a way to make sense of the violence that we endured. These vulnerable and conflicting feelings emerge as a form of testing the waters. We hope to find camaraderie or someone to tell us that what our families did was normal.

Additionally, those of us—children, parents, people—who lived in families struggling to survive in the system through anti-Blackness, poverty, welfare, homelessness, prisons, and xenophobia can hold a sort of badge of honor for these childhood beatings and psychological games. We must make sense of it to survive—create something honorable, throw in a bit of comic relief.

The funny thing about cycles is that they keep going and going until there is a break. We often awaken to the reality of our struggles as we move from children to the role of parent, sometimes without interrupting the cycle of pain. We may see the mirror images of our parents looking back at us as we raise a hand, increase the volume of our voice, belittle or isolate our children. The comic conversations and the glitches are the catalysts helping us to shift our stories, grieve our past, and heal ourselves and ultimately our relations.

Who am I?

I often describe my childhood as a labyrinth of confusion, requiring years of adulthood to untangle its intricacies. I recall the moment I seemingly emerged into consciousness, finding myself alongside my mother, our roles magically clear: she the caretaker, and I the cared for.

The rules of my role were etched into me. I reluctantly and fearfully followed. Where am I? What is my purpose? What should I do? I never had much time to answer the questions. The responses were already waiting for me. Life was seamlessly thought up by the adults around me. My role involved order, paying attention, and following rules. My siblings and I were told to follow the rules, oftentimes with no explanation. There was little reason beyond "I am your mother" or father or other adult in charge of keeping me safe. Safe from what,

I never quite understood, but keeping me safe was apparently one of their most important goals.

I suppose my parents were confused as well. Desperate to fit in, learn the language, provide, and survive. My parents navigated the welfare system, police surveillance, and the medical industrial complex with fear at the steering wheel. Fear of losing us to the state. Fear of getting cut off of welfare. Fear that my mother's disability would lead others to deem her an unstable mother. My parents carried this weight, and it spilled over often. I had been deep in the vision of my own pain, but I hadn't yet seen the well-formulated keloids my parents carried.

Systems like family policing reinforce and justify parenting from a place of authority. The very systems that have punished parents become the tools we use to punish our children.

For years, my focus on healing revolved around the psychological and sexual violence inflicted by my sister during my childhood and teenage years. It wasn't until some five years ago that I began to delve into the influence of my upbringing. As I persist in my mission to prevent and eradicate childhood sexual abuse and all forms of sexual violence, I've gained profound insights. The trauma I endured continues to haunt me, permeating every aspect of my life. I've come to understand its impact on my failed relationships, lack of boundaries, and sexual issues. Initially, I failed to recognize how the strictness of my upbringing contributed to my survival of child sexual abuse. The grooming, boundary violations, and uncomfortable encounters were facilitated by the family's controlling environment. My mother's absolute authority over my life—dictating my attire, hygiene, social circle, and even emotions—laid the groundwork for dynamics of control, stifled curiosity, and suppressed instincts. This rigid parent-child dichotomy echoes the legacy of colonialism, prioritizing efficiency and order over our innate humanity.

Who's a family?

Historically marginalized family structures (including single-parent, female-headed, queer, and polyamorous) have slowly gained some visibility and recognition within mainstream spaces. This expanding definition of family acknowledges the diverse ways in which individuals form intimate bonds and create supportive networks.

An example of this shift can be seen in the growing recognition—largely due to feminists and queer folks—of chosen families. Formed through deep emotional connections rather than biological or legal ties, chosen families often consist of individuals who support and care for each other as kin. Chosen families may include close friends, mentors, or community members who provide the love and support typically associated with traditional family units.

Yet despite the power of the chosen family, the family policing system plays a vital role to shape, strengthen, and perpetuate the concept of the "American family." Laws, policies, and systems establish and validate the idea of a nuclear family. Some examples of this regulation include same-sex marriage legislation, public housing policies, abortion laws, and child welfare and custody laws. However, this narrow definition of family has always marginalized people of color, particularly Black, Indigenous, and economically disadvantaged families, as well as families with a single parent or those formed through adoption.

Over time, the composition and understanding of family has shifted significantly, reflecting demands from broader cultural and social movements including feminism and queer liberation. This evolution has primarily aimed to create a more expansive and inclusive definition of family, accommodating diverse familial structures and relationships. Reproductive technologies (often restricted to those with resources or supportive health care) have further challenged traditional notions of biological kinship, allowing individuals to pursue parenthood through surrogacy, sperm or egg donation, and adoption regardless of their sexual orientation, gender, or marital status.

By embracing diverse family configurations and challenging outdated norms, we create space for all individuals to experience love, belonging, and support within familial relationships.

Or do we?

◆

Despite these endeavors to adjust and reconfigure family dynamics, the entrenched social frameworks maintaining traditional norms frequently evade scrutiny and resistance.

In precolonial societies, familial structures were deeply entwined with communal and kinship bonds. Families fulfilled various roles, including production, socialization, and mutual assistance. Their function was closely tied to subsistence tasks such as farming, hunting, and gathering, where all family members contributed to collective survival efforts. Thus, precolonial family dynamics were fundamentally aligned with the land and nature.

Being in right relationship with the land involves acknowledging and respecting the deep connections between humans and the natural environment. This perspective embodies a deep respect for the land, its ecosystems, and all the living beings it sustains. From Indigenous perspectives, this concept often involves understanding the land as a living entity with its own rights and consciousness. At the heart of this relationship is the idea of taking care of the land in a responsible way for the benefit of both present and future generations. This means using methods that support the long-term health and well-being of the environment, such as conserving resources and finding ways to restore what has been lost.

Postcolonial family structures, on the other hand, underwent significant transformations due to the imposition of colonial rule and the introduction of capitalist economic systems. The family policing system was an integral part of the settler-colonial nation-building project of the United States. The family policing system stole Indigenous children from families and attacked Indigenous kinship structures. Colonialism reshaped traditional Indigenous communities by replacing communal land tenure systems with individual land ownership and wage labor, which also served to justify the colonizers' theft of land. Nuclear and patriarchal family units prioritized participation in market-oriented activities. Consequently, Indigenous families were forced to shift their focus toward serving as labor units for capitalist production, with household members engaging in wage-earning work to sustain themselves.

The creation of family structures was heavily influenced by the imperatives of capitalist expansion, labor exploitation, and social control, a foundational tenet of the family policing system.

Children were taken from immigrant families to work for white settlers, with little questioning of the fact that this was exploitative. To the contrary, taking children from their parents to work for white settlers was touted as safety and upward mobility. Families became vital units for replenishing the labor force, maintaining social stability, and perpetuating capitalist modes of production. The drive for profit reshaped the dynamics of familial relationships, emphasizing economic success over traditional communal values.

Essentially, our connections to the land, animals, ourselves, and our families underwent a profound transformation. The communal container of precolonial societies shifted toward a profit-driven model in which success is measured by financial gain.

What's love got to do with it?

I'm uncertain if my parents were ever truly in love, or if they even liked each other. Their dynamic was often obscured by the strains of life. Arguments were commonplace, as in any typical marriage. I sensed my mother's disappointment in my father's shortcomings, while my father seemed burdened by his perceived inadequacies. We lived under a veil of secrecy, cautious not to divulge family matters to outsiders, especially welfare authorities. We had to remain vigilant, ready to conceal my father's presence at a moment's notice to avoid being officially unrecognized as poor and thus ineligible for state aid.

Straddling the line between pre- and postcolonial family dynamics, my immediate family, along with aunts and cousins, formed our tribe. We resided in tenement buildings, scattered across the second to fifth floors. Amid the chaos, my fondest memories are of the bonds formed with my cousins. Together, we navigated the challenges of childhood, finding solace and companionship in each other's presence. In a world that discouraged outside friendships, my cousins became my anchor, providing a sense of belonging.

Despite adults' attempts to explain love, it remained elusive and incomprehensible. Its nature was undefined, with the promise that one day, we would grasp its meaning. In this system, families are tasked with guiding children toward achieving dominant ideals of success, love, and happiness. How can parents teach love to their children? I don't believe it can be directly taught. Love is something that must be experienced. However, in our society, adhering to certain markers or "bullet points" of love seems to guide us toward our perceived life goals—our partners, families, and careers.

However, reconciling these ideals with the realities of family life can be challenging, particularly when the notion of enduring romance clashes with the complexities of everyday existence. Romantic love is often viewed as the cornerstone of a legitimate family structure, adhering to heterosexual norms. Yet the presence or absence of this love can significantly impact the family's perceived success. Shifting the focus from tangible concepts like survival to fleeting emotions like romance places a heavy burden on individuals, as the success or failure of the family becomes contingent on personal choices rather than broader institutions.

Notions such as "I'm bad at love" or "I'm no good at relationships" highlight the shift toward personal responsibility for the family's success. Divorce or single parenthood are shamed and discouraged at any cost. Gendered roles further complicate matters, with social expectations dictating how individuals should navigate romantic relationships to fulfill hegemonic norms. Think "men are from Mars; women are from Venus." These deeply ingrained ideas often lead individuals to strive for inclusion within systems that may not fully acknowledge or represent them. Once integrated into these systems, individuals may inadvertently adopt characteristics perpetuating a cycle of conformity.

Capitalism, colonialism, and heteropatriarchy have long depended on the idea of romantic heterosexual love and marriage. First, marriage acts as a way to control society, enforcing traditional gender roles and ensuring a steady supply of workers. Women take on unpaid household chores and childcare, freeing men to work in the capitalist economy. Second, marriage helps maintain economic stability by consolidating wealth and property within families and across generations. It also fuels consumerism, with weddings and related industries driving spending. Third, colonialism imposed Western ideas of love and marriage on colonized peoples, erasing Indigenous values and ways of life. These myths and violent systems uphold power structures, reinforce gender norms, and fuel economic exploitation, all while promoting the idea that romantic love is essential for happiness and success.

The kids

In addition to romantic love, society primes everyone to pedestal white childbirth as a way to perpetuate patriarchy. This hyper-valorized version of childbirth does not match the material experiences of a birthing body who is Black, brown, queer, or poor, which often exposes structural failures around bodily autonomy, reproduction, or care. This tension between rhetoric and reality breeds feelings of failure or inadequacy. Children born out of wedlock or conceived through violence or casual encounters often face stigma and societal judgment, generating feelings of worthlessness or self-hatred among parents and children. These structural failings lead to and perpetuate real interpersonal harm.

Within this settler-colonial construct, the role of children is primarily viewed as preparatory. Parents are told to guide them through socialization processes to navigate educational systems, pursue higher education, enter the workforce, marry, and have children, perpetuating a cycle of dominant norms and expectations. Actions align with the structures, and therefore children are often treated as possessions or territories to be colonized by parents. This mindset leads to surveillance, control, punishment, and even disownment, all under the guise of ensuring the child's well-being and success in life. The pressure to conform to traditional roles and the lack of recognition for children's rights contribute to a culture in which abuse can be hidden and unaddressed, ultimately supporting the cycle of abuse within the family structure.

The family policing system says that it intervenes on behalf of children. However, it is the building block of surveillance. Judges oversee parents and literally assume a parental authority of children and parents via legal doctrines. Caseworkers, social workers, and the web of mandated reporters are told to ignore what the children want, and instead do what they think is best. In sum, the very people who conceptualize themselves as child savers abandon the children they purport to protect. They not only adopt the narrative of authoritarianism, they are the authority. They are a part of the cycle of control.

However, a growing movement challenges this paradigm and advocates a different approach to parenting. A call to decolonize and rehumanize. A call for mindful parenting, recognizing children's autonomy, and fostering environments that embrace diversity and difference. This movement is often led by people, particularly children, who do not fit into prescribed roles. Gender-variant children, deaf and hard-of-hearing children navigating hearing families without sign language, and individuals with autism and other neurodivergent conditions are essential voices in promoting acceptance of diverse language and cognitive processes and challenging misconceptions about what is considered "normal."

These movements strive to create safer environments for children who have historically been marginalized or deemed uncontrollable by the family policing system. Such children may not conform to prescribed gender roles or hegemonic expectations of productivity, leading to their isolation, shame, or even abuse at the hands of adults who are conditioned by the system to enforce conformity for their children's perceived benefit and survival.

Transgender children often face significant challenges in environments that strictly enforce traditional gender roles. For instance, a transgender child who identifies as a different gender from the one assigned at birth might be subjected to harsh disciplinary actions, conversion therapy, or exclusion from social and educational opportunities. These punitive measures are often justified under the guise of protecting the child or ensuring their "normal" development, but they instead inflict deep psychological harm and hinder the child's ability to thrive. Transgender children face increased scrutiny and intervention from child welfare services, which operate under a framework that often fails to recognize or support gender diversity.

Recognizing these parallels provides insights into the workings of power within society, whether at the macro level of colonization or the micro level of familial relationships.

Policing, how?

Parental figures often assume roles as enforcers, overseers, and disciplinarians. Through this process, families serve as training grounds, preparing individuals to navigate and thrive within colonial and capitalistic societal structures by instilling obedience, conformity, and achievement of predetermined milestones.

Families, in their pursuit of conformity, may resort to authoritarian methods, stripping individuals of their agency. A family can shape and normalize how we police each other. Colonial structures permeate our family dynamics and normalize abusive behaviors. A culture of silencing of survivors protects these practices, as those who speak out and name the violence in a family structure are often gaslighted or blamed for their trauma. Such policing fosters an environment ripe for emotional abuse, physical violence, and psychological harm.

The imposition of rigid gender roles further exacerbates these dynamics, dictating expectations for behavior, career paths, and relationships. Personal expression and lifestyle choices are tightly regulated, with deviations from norms often met with disapproval or punishment. Individuals may endure emotional manipulation, verbal abuse, or even physical violence as a means of enforcing compliance.

This control extends beyond overt actions to subtler forms of coercion and manipulation. Emotional blackmail, guilt-tripping, and gaslighting are commonly employed tactics to maintain power dynamics within the family. Under the guise of protection or guidance, family members suppress individual autonomy and enforce conformity.

The trauma of childhood influences self-perception and decision-making, shaping relationships with friends, romantic partners, and colleagues. The policing inherent in many traditional family structures significantly impacts caregiving. We learn that relationships are not about curiosity and care but about a fastidious compatibility checklist or about ownership and the reproduction of colonial ideals. In the pursuit of finding a life partner and potentially starting a family, individuals often confront the realities of these learned familial dynamics.

Redefining family

Black people have always had to redefine family. With a tradition of caring for each other informally, Black families take in children who are not their own. Shifts in traditional gender roles continue to reshape family dynamics. Queer people and other marginalized people also inhabit nonnormative family structures. Economic considerations such as housing affordability and job stability shape decisions about marriage and childbirth and kinship and household formations. These shifts are no longer shaping the minority of families. The dominant culture is starting to reflect this reality. Many individuals choose to delay or reject marriage and childbirth to pursue higher education, establish careers, and prioritize personal development and joy.

People living their lives continue to redefine the family. Now let's dream about what this could do. Could this configuration of the family offer the possibility for connection, deep love, and care? Imagine a space for genuine experience and growth, guided by curiosity rather than judgment. Cultivating family within this paradigm involves embracing feelings, thoughts, and actions as opportunities for learning and growth, supported by community and familial bonds. This future is not just a utopian vision—it's within reach.

We must actively explore new ways of connecting with each other, embracing a multitude of possibilities. How did your family express care or love? How did power or control show up? What is the current intentional function of your family? How can we support each other in decolonizing our relations? How can we transition from assimilation to authentic existence?

Social and political movements contribute to the realization of this dream—Black Lives Matter, Indigenous people's movements, transgender liberation, feminist organizing, disability and healing justice, abolition demands, climate justice, children's liberation, and more. As these movements gain momentum, we inch toward the process of decolonization, bringing us closer to a world where healing, freedom, and authentic connections thrive.

#Heal2End

Most of us consider institutions, structures, and oppressive systems—for example the government, religious organizations, the medical industrial complex, the criminal justice system, and the educational system—as distant and external. However, to begin to heal it is crucial to recognize the role of the traditional postcolonial family as an institution that can perpetuate harm and enact the work of the punitive or carceral state.

I've stopped participating in the retelling of "funny stories" about the punishments my parents administered. I no longer seek solace in shared tales of pain and suffering. I've begun recognizing the underlying patterns, allowing myself to feel the anger and sorrow inherent in this experience. The need for my mother's recognition and apology has faded, replaced by compassion.

As I grow to understand the cycle of harm enacted by my family through the ideas of child protection and rearing, I acknowledge that my family members were trapped in the cycle too. My healing is, in part, what many members of my family could not access, those who followed the rules set forth in this system of family policing. I recognize the systemic pressures they faced, I see how the weight of expectations and punitive measures shaped their actions. Their choices were often driven by survival within a rigid framework that allowed little room for deviation. This realization has deepened my empathy, as I understand that their participation in these harmful cycles was not a matter of choice but necessity.

I navigate complexities as I heal from the harm inflicted by my parents, compounded by institutions (religious, educational, medical) and enforced by the family policing system. My journey in healing, therefore, is not only about addressing personal wounds but also about disentangling the broader systemic and institutional threads that have contributed to this harm. The journey toward healing involves unraveling the layers of indoctrination and oppression woven into familial relationships.

6

Who Do You Tell?

Shannon Perez-Darby

---

*These are true stories with names and identifying details
changed to protect the anonymity of survivors.*

What do we do when a child experiences sexual violence? Who do
we tell? We are told to "just make a report." We are told that the
system will help. In my twenty years of anti-violence advocacy, I
have never once seen the system make things better for a survivor.

I was twenty-three years old, fleeing a relationship that had
crushed me. I didn't call myself a survivor, not at first. I knew the
relationship was bad—everyone knew it was bad. I hadn't slept
through the night once since we moved in together. There were
always sleepless nights—drinking, a fight, a crisis, sex. I knew we
couldn't coexist in that same big-small city where all the queers
knew each other and there were no social places where I wouldn't
have to see him. He had stalked me, and no matter what I tried, I

couldn't stop him from coming into the coffee shop where I worked and pretending that he didn't know me. Every place I reached out to for help didn't know how to help me. Not knowing what else to do, I left the state.

Fortunately, as I was leaving, I was offered my dream job working as the youth advocate at one of the few LGBTQ-specific domestic violence programs in the United States. As community-based domestic violence advocates, we weren't therapists, we weren't social workers, we were peer survivors supporting people experiencing violence in their own self-determination and safety. As queer and trans survivors of domestic and sexual violence, we knew the crushing nature of this violence. As survivors, we understood what it was to have your sense of self slowly chipped away. And we knew precisely what it was like to wake up one day, years into an abusive relationship, twisted into knots and unaware of how the violence started or how to get out.

In 2005, when I started my anti-violence advocacy, there were almost no domestic violence programs directly supporting young people. Young people might receive support from a program but only as the children of adult survivors. Young people weren't the center of the support—they were there because of the harm a parent had experienced.

Young people deserve to be supported beyond what they may witness between adults in their households. Child sexual abuse is an epidemic. Over half of women and almost one in three men have experienced sexual violence during their lifetimes, while more than four in five female rape survivors report that they were first raped before age twenty-five and almost half were first raped as a minor (that is, before the age of eighteen).[1]

Where adults would reach out and "cold call" our advocacy line, youth rarely did. In my ten years as a youth advocate, I could count on my fingers the number of people under the age of eighteen who called our advocacy line without a prior connection with a youth advocate. We went to them. We started talking to young people about their friends, families, and relationships, and they talked to us about violence.

One day, years into being a youth advocate, the principal of Capitol Lake High School (CLHS; the name has been changed to protect the anonymity of the people involved), an alternative school in my community, called to let us know that one of their students had been sexually assaulted, and, as a school, they wanted to help but didn't know how. A couple of hours later, I was at the school. The principal introduced me to Amanda and her classmate Maria.

Amanda, who was sixteen, had been sexually assaulted by a teenage girl she had been dating. Amanda was shy and wanted to move slowly into this new relationship. The girl she was dating hadn't listened. Amanda said no, the girlfriend pushed things, ignored Amanda's requests to stop, and sexually assaulted Amanda. After the assault, the girl ended the relationship. Amanda was confused, overwhelmed, and unsure what to do. She told her best friend, Maria, what happened, and together they reached out to a trusted adult at the school.

The friendship of teenage girls can be so powerful. When I was a teenager, my friends were my entire world. There were four of us in total, and we were loyal and committed friends. Sexual violence was the constant reality of our teenage lives. I remember almost nothing from middle school except the tightening of my entire body when, in the lunchroom, in front of everyone, another middle schooler, a boy, reached over and grabbed my butt. I froze, my heart beating in my chest and a ringing in my ears. All I could hear was the laughing of this boy and his friends. He had violated my body. In front of everyone. No one said or did a thing. I told no one.

There was the constant safety planning with a friend whose creepy stepfather we always tried to avoid. He had a special room in the basement where he painted areola and pubic hair onto Barbies and hung naked lady calendars on the walls. He insisted we watch *Death Race 2000*, a 1970s dystopian movie with a road race to the death, in the spirit of the *Hunger Games* books. The film featured nude women, sex, violence, misogyny. The stepfather insisted on sitting there and watching it all with us. We were thirteen.

Years later, during our senior year in high school, this same friend told us that she had been changing clothes in the shared bathroom of her home one day and discovered a video camera hidden under some towels. It was recording her while she changed. She told her mother, and handed over the video camera. Her mother watched the tape, told our friend she would take care of it, and they never spoke about it again. Our friend knew in her gut that something was wrong. She did the only other thing she knew to do—she talked to her trusted friends. So, we safety planned, although we did not know this term at the time. We made plans for her to be at one of our houses as much as possible, or for one or more of us to go home with her after school. We reorganized our lives to help her stay safe.

We knew we needed help. We talked through the various adults we could ask and landed on a teacher whom all of us liked. When I think back to the decision now, I'm curious about our choice. He wasn't the most empathetic or emotionally intelligent teacher. He was a bit gruff and frank, but he was also funny. I think we picked him because he was the only adult we knew who openly broke the rules. He would loudly proclaim that he was veering off the approved curriculum. He was my only teacher who tried to teach practical things he thought we might need but would likely not be taught. He taught me financial literacy, including how to open up a bank account and balance a checkbook (this was the '90s, when people still balanced their checkbooks). One day in class he told us to close our textbooks and marched us out to the parking lot. "Who has a car here?" he yelled. A classmate raised her hand, and he taught us how to change a tire and check the oil. I still think about this teacher every time I have to change a tire.

One day after school a couple of us hung back and told him what had happened. He was clearly freaked out. I don't remember exactly what he said, but I do remember how it made me feel. I knew immediately that he had nothing to offer. I could feel how desperately he wanted the conversation to be over. We told him—and nothing happened. We told—and there was no help. No calls were made, no resource was offered, no strategies were discussed. We had only each other for safety.

◆

When the Capitol Lake High principal initially reached out to us about the violence Amanda had experienced, he had a number of concerns. He knew in his gut that making a mandated report would only hurt Amanda, and he was concerned about his role as a person required to report harms against minors to the authorities (also known as a "mandated reporter"). In general, when an adult causes harm to a young person, mandated reporters are required to report to child protective services, but if violence happens between two people under the age of eighteen, in most of the United States, mandated reporters are required to make a report directly to law enforcement. Which is to say, you're required to call the cops regardless of what the person experiencing violence wants.

Most survivors do not report sexual assaults: 63 percent of adult sexual assaults are not reported to police, and only 12 percent of child sexual abuse is report to the authorities.[2] There are so many reasons people do not report the violence they experience to the police. We know in part it's because the police simply aren't helpful and that, for many survivors, the fear of criminalization is a very real threat.[3] Nearly 60 percent of women in state prisons nationwide have a history of physical or sexual abuse before being incarcerated, with 37 percent of those women stating the violence they experienced happened before they were eighteen.[4]

What survivors need is support, connection, and resources. Policing isn't about providing resources or support. Policing is about getting information to see if a "crime" has occurred and gathering evidence of that crime for the purpose of a potential prosecution. Police are not neutral observers listening to survivors with the goal of supporting their self-determination. Police are agents of the state. What survivors need is to be supported in their safety and self-determination. Police investigate crimes. These are very different tasks.

Experiencing sexual violence can feel so disempowering. Sexual violence is precisely about not being in charge of your body. What survivors of sexual violence need is support to restore their sense of autonomy. Everyone needs this, but no one more so than young people. So many adults are conditioned to orient themselves paternalistically to young people. Many adults treat young people with disrespect and believe that young people should not get to make decisions about their own bodies. This logic perpetuates rape culture—that is, the values and practices that normalize sexual violence. Rape culture is many things, including the normalization of coercive sex or school dress codes that tell teenage girls that they must wear long skirts and ban "spaghetti strap tops" and visible bra straps. These norms make teenage girls' bodies the problem and condition girls to believe that it is their responsibility to prevent men from looking at their bodies rather than making men and boys responsible for their own behavior. Paternalism perpetuates rape culture by telling children that someone else is in charge of their bodies.

Nothing magical happens on the day a person turns eighteen. A person does not instantly gain new skills or a grounded sense of power. Being a skillful, grounded, autonomous adult comes from being a skillful, grounded, autonomous young person. Our task as adults who want to support young people is to create safe environments for them to explore and try out who they want to be in the world. Young people should have the dignity of experimentation, an essential pathway to learn about oneself.

And of course we shouldn't put adult expectations on young people. Whenever I talk about youth self-determination, I can feel the panic arise in people. "But what if their lack of experience means they get hurt?" or "It's not fair. We shouldn't make young people responsible for adult decisions." And I agree. Young people shouldn't have to make adult decisions. The space between autonomous adult decisions and youth self-determination is vast. Spend time with any four-year-old, and you can see how they already assert their own bodily autonomy. Support them with language and choice, and they'll tell you whom they want to hug, whether the water is too warm or too cold, whether they want water or milk, whether the pressure of the washcloth is too hard or too soft. These are the ways we build the muscle of self-determination in young people. It's not appropriate for a seven-year-old to have to understand the nuances of child protective services or criminal legal consequences. Those are not kid decisions. But it's very appropriate for a seven-year-old to decide which people they do and don't want to hug at the family reunion.

The principal and staff at Capitol Lake High School were amazing. At every turn, their question was "What's the right thing to do? How can we support what Amanda wants?" They were never driven by questions of liability. They never asked, "How can we not get in trouble?" While they did want to understand the legal landscape of reporting, at the end of the day they cared most about doing right by Amanda. In my ten years of working directly with young people experiencing violence, this was the only time leaders at an institution reached out to ask, "How do we do right by this young person?" and not "What is our liability here?"

In polite conversation, everyone will tell you, "Of course, we care about young people. Of course, we care what survivors want." But that is not how people act in private. In the privacy of their offices, many organizational leaders are driven by questions of liability and compliance. I am forever grateful for the administrators at Capitol Lake, who modeled what adults can do to support the self-determination of young people experiencing violence.

What did Amanda want?

Amanda told me that she wanted to report the rape. She told me that she was afraid this girl would harm other people, and she wanted someone to know. I talked to her about her relationship with the police. Was she afraid of the police? Did she see them as helpful or hurtful? What did she want to happen as a result of calling the police? What was she afraid might happen?

Amanda was afraid that her parents would find out. She was not out to them, and she didn't think they would "be cool" knowing that she was queer. We talked for a long time about balancing the risk of her parents finding out she was queer with her desire to report what had happened. At the end of the day, she still wanted to report.

In general, mandatory reporters are not required to make reports to young people's parents. As a domestic violence advocate, I had a confidential relationship with Amanda, so I could share the information she shared with me only with her explicit, written permission or when legally required by our state's mandatory reporting laws to report to child protective services or the police. We talked through the options. Amanda could make the call herself while Maria and I were in the room. Amanda could be in charge of exactly what was said but not have to do it alone. Or I could make the report with her in the room. We would talk about what I would say ahead of time, so she would know how her story would be shared. She wouldn't have to make the call, but she would hear exactly what was said. Or I could make the report alone and report back to her about what happened. We would still talk about what I would say, but she wouldn't have to be in the room while I made the call. It was her choice. She chose the last option.

As a mandatory reporter, I am not an investigator for the state. It is not my job to gather information to be a better reporter. As an advocate, it is my job to listen to survivors, help them understand options, and whenever possible, help to remove institutional barriers.

Amanda and I had just met that day, and we spoke for about an hour. When it came time to make the report that Amanda had requested, I knew her first name, her school, and the information she'd shared about the sexual assault she'd experienced. I called the nonemergency police line to share what we had discussed. It took less than five minutes. A couple of days later, I followed up with Amanda to see how she was doing. She told me that, even though I had shared only her first name and school, the evening after we made the report, police officers showed up at Amanda's house, told her parents what happened, outed her, and as a result she was kicked out of her house for being gay. The system did not keep Amanda safe. The system made things worse.

People shut down when faced with domestic and sexual violence. Domestic and sexual violence continues because of our collective inability to face the harm we are capable of doing to each other. When we talk about children being abused, people become despondent. I see the look in people's eyes—they are a thousand miles away. To live in a world where children experience massive rates of sexual violence is a reality that most of us find intolerable. And it is intolerable. We should be outraged. If every person on this planet could truly take in the scale of harm, the reality of sexual violence so many children are experiencing, it would be a global emergency. The urgency to act would be undeniable. But to act would mean to fundamentally shift our societies. We can change the conditions that lead to domestic and sexual violence. To end domestic and sexual violence we need the end of structural oppression. We need a universal basic income. We need an investment in truly affordable housing. We need to examine our own role in setting up and maintaining rape culture. We need to practice being in right relationships with ourselves and our communities.

For many, these changes feel too big for us as individuals to face, so instead we do nothing. We make reports with the vague hope that *someone* will do *something*. We convince ourselves that picking up the phone and making a report means we've done our duty. We convince ourselves that the professionals will handle it. But this is not working.

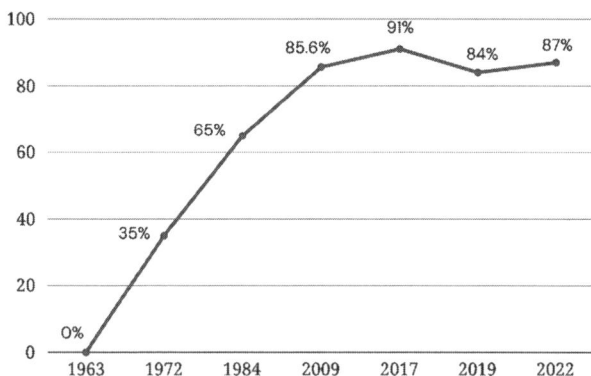

National Percentage of Unsubstantiated Reports, 1963–2022, US Department of Health and Human Services, Administration for Children and Families

Family policing systems were put in place in large part as a response to the Child Abuse Prevention and Treatment Act (CAPTA) enacted in 1974.[5] CAPTA is the federal legislation that dictates mandatory reporting and child welfare practices, and its associated federal funding, across the United States. Since these systems were enacted, the rates of unsubstantiated reports of abuse and neglect have increased significantly. Unsubstantiated reports are cases in which a report was made but the investigating agency either couldn't follow up on the report or followed up and could not verify the claims made in the report.

In 1972, before CAPTA was adopted, 610,000 child abuse or neglect reports were made nationally. Of those reports an estimated 35 percent were found to be unsubstantiated. Now, fifty years into our current mandatory reporting systems, we see unsubstantiated rates between 84 percent and 91 percent. In 2022, there was a total of 4.3 million reports nationally, with only half of those cases (2.1 million) being investigated. Of the nearly 2 million investigated cases in 2022, 558,899 children were deemed to have experienced abuse or neglect, with a total unsubstantiated rate of 87 percent.[6] In other words, the vast majority of reports made to family policing systems are deemed inactionable by that system. More reporting does not necessarily mean an increase in support for young people experiencing harm.

"But what about the children?!"

Instead of facing the real harms children experience, never-ending moral panics create false specters that obscure the real nature of violence. These moral panics tell highly racialized stories about the dangerous strangers who will kidnap your children. They tell us that we should be afraid of outsiders and require carceral solutions like punishment and criminalization. Many claim that our children will be safe with better laws and law enforcement. We are told that if we can just incarcerate the "bad men," children will be safe. This lie is the foundation on which real harm to children is perpetuated.

Children are most likely to be abused by someone they know. Of child abuse and neglect cases reported to child welfare organizations nationally, 98.5 percent of the people causing harm were known to the children who were harmed.[7] Of sexual abuse cases reported to law enforcement, 93 percent of victims under the age of eighteen knew the person who harmed them.[8] Young people are most likely to be harmed by their family, friends, and acquaintances. To face the fact that those who are mostly likely to be abusive are not strangers plucking children off the streets but familiar people means facing our own complacency in violence.

Dominant culture teaches young people that their bodies are not their own. We tell young people they must unequivocally listen to adults, even at the cost of their dignity and safety. Every adult I know has a memory of not being believed as a child. Every adult I know has had the experience of being young, of knowing something that felt deeply true to them, and having an adult tell them they were wrong. When the self-determination of youth is not honored, young people learn the conditions of self-betrayal that make them vulnerable to abuse. It's much easier to manipulate and harm someone who has been taught that their intuition is insignificant and that they don't have a say over what happens to their bodies. "But children are not adults," they shout. "Of course, we need to tell children what to do. How else will they learn?"

We can honor the bodily autonomy of young people and provide safe, age-appropriate spaces to learn and grow. What every survivor of any age needs is support being in their body. They need support to understand what they experienced. They need support to know it wasn't their fault. Every survivor needs to be heard and held by their community. If we don't respect children, if we can't listen to children, how can we support their survival?

Our world is filled with sexual violence, high on mandatory reporting but low on support. We must end family policing and mandatory reporting—not because we don't care about the harm young people experience, but precisely because we do. We deeply care when *anyone* has experienced harm. To build a world free from domestic and sexual violence is to build a world where young people can talk about the violence they're experiencing and they are heard and believed. It's a world where every person has their basic needs met, with access to stable housing, food, clean water, and community. It is a world where the autonomy of young people is so ingrained that we would never think to act on their behalf without asking, "What do you want?" It's a world where we don't need systems of reporting, because everyone has strong, resourced communities, a world where children talk and we listen.

7

The Community Dimensions
of State Child Protection

Dorothy Roberts

———————

The US child welfare system, the institution charged with protecting
children from abuse and neglect, is marked by alarming racial disparities.[1] Black and Native American children are overrepresented in
the national foster care population.[2] Black children make up nearly
a quarter of the national foster care population, but represent less
than 15 percent of all American children.[3] Eleven percent of Black
children and 15 percent of Native American children can expect to
enter the foster care system before they turn eighteen.[4] Children of
color are also disproportionately represented in the foster care system compared to white children. For example, Black children are
twice as likely to enter the system as white children.[5]

This chapter has been adapted from a previously published article: Dorothy E. Roberts, "The
Community Dimension of State Child Protection," *Hofstra Law Review* 34, no. 1 (2005).

The color of child welfare is most apparent in big cities with sizable minoritized and foster care populations. In Cook County, Illinois, home to Chicago, nearly 70 percent of children in foster care are Black.[6] At the end of 2023, 50 percent of the children in foster care in New York City were Black, while only 5 percent were white.[7] Similar disparities exist in states with smaller minoritized populations. As of 2023, Native American children in Minnesota are sixteen times more likely than white children to be placed in foster care, and Black children in the state are twice as likely.[8]

When I began researching racial disparities in the child welfare system over twenty years ago, I found myself in conversation with a civil liberties lawyer and mentioned that, at the time, in Washington State 10 percent of all Native American children were in foster care.[9] "Oh my God," she exclaimed. "One out of ten children in Washington are in foster care. That's unbelievable!" "No," I corrected, "not ten percent of *all* children, ten percent of *Native American* children." "Oh, I see," she replied, her alarm dissipating. Of course, the figure was just as disturbing for the Native American communities in Washington that experience such extreme state disruption of their families.[10] But this community impact of state child protection is virtually invisible in legal, sociological, and social work research on the child welfare system and the importance of communities to child development. Just as the impact of this statistic disappeared from this socially conscious lawyer's mind when associated with children of color rather than white children, it remains strangely unnoticed by researchers and policymakers.

In this essay, I explore the connections between communities and child welfare that researchers and policymakers recognize and those they fail to see. Why are some aspects of communities' relationship to child welfare more prominent in research and policy than others? Social scientists' growing interest in neighborhood effects on child development has coincided with social workers embracing community-based child welfare approaches. However, these neighborhood-oriented approaches to child welfare are too narrow and ignore the damaging impact of the child welfare system itself on neighborhoods experiencing high rates of involvement by child protective services. I discuss how disciplinary and philosophical blinders obscure this dimension of state child protection from scholars and practitioners and propose a research agenda that investigates the community-level impact of the spatial concentration of child welfare agency involvement in marginalized neighborhoods.

Community-based child welfare research

It is now recognized that communities affect children's development, well-being, and life chances.[11] The traditional African adage "It takes a village to raise a child" is a mantra of child welfare discourse. We take for granted that growing up in a well-resourced neighborhood is better for children than growing up in a disinvested one. Research confirms this intuition by studying neighborhood effects—the impact of poverty, unemployment, and residential instability, as well as community-level social dynamics—on children and families.[12]

William Julius Wilson pioneered this research in *The Truly Disadvantaged*, demonstrating how urban deindustrialization in the 1970s resulted in an extreme concentration of poverty and unemployment in African American neighborhoods.[13] Residents of these neighborhoods experienced "concentration effects" that imposed burdens beyond those caused by their individual and family characteristics.[14] Researchers have since theorized and measured how the concentration of social and economic disadvantage in urban neighborhoods affects residents.[15] Noting that child-related problems "tend to come bundled together at the neighborhood level," these studies examine how neighborhood social composition and processes influence childhood well-being.[16]

A body of research explores how living in a disadvantaged neighborhood creates health and behavior problems for children. The influential Project on Human Development in Chicago Neighborhoods underscored the impact of "social disorganization" and "collective efficacy," or neighbors' shared belief in their ability to take joint action on behalf of children's welfare. The project found that neighborhoods with high levels of collective efficacy experienced fewer incidents of violence and personal victimization. Researchers argued that collective efficacy mediated the effects of poverty and residential instability on violence.[17]

Community approaches to child welfare practice

Social work theorists and practitioners have increasingly adopted community-based approaches to child welfare decision-making, inspired in part by research linking communities and children's welfare.[18] Though community approaches to social work remain on the fringe of typical child welfare practice, community-based initiatives are taking hold in pilot projects across the country and in theorizing about the future of social work.

Some of these initiatives integrate communities into traditional casework, investigating child maltreatment and providing services to individual clients.[19] These programs claim to draw on the strengths of families and communities, try to respect cultural norms, and initiate partnerships with existing neighborhood organizations.[20] They may acknowledge a responsibility to communities by consulting with neighborhood leaders and stakeholders in setting policy and designing services. As one advocate describes, "Community social work draws on and contributes to the resources of the community in dealing with problems."[21]

Other programs operate as an alternative or supplement to child welfare agencies by building neighborhood capacity to provide healthier environments for children.[22] Recognizing that reforming child welfare is inadequate to reverse the devastating consequences of neighborhood disadvantage, these initiatives seek to transform the social fabric of poor communities by improving schools, increasing safety, creating jobs, mobilizing civic engagement, and expanding resources for families.[23] Under this approach, communities themselves are the organizing principle of child welfare interventions.[24]

The system's community impact

Social scientists examine the community characteristics that affect child welfare, and social work theorists, funders, and practitioners have begun to incorporate these findings in their work.[25] However, neither group has identified the child welfare system itself as a neighborhood characteristic with community-wide impact. Social scientists have yet significantly to investigate the sociopolitical impact of the spatial concentration of child welfare supervision in marginalized neighborhoods. Likewise, theorists consider communities when prescribing child welfare policies, but do not recognize how child welfare agencies affect communities.

To the extent that neighborhood researchers consider the role of local institutions, they typically view them as positive resources for residents countering neighborhood disorganization.[26] Robert Sampson, a Chicago neighborhood project researcher, argues that institutions like neighborhood associations, churches, and schools "reflect the structural embodiment of community cohesion."[27] However, it remains unclear the extent to which intense institutional policing of families by child welfare agencies affects collective efficacy.

Since 2000, researchers and state welfare departments have investigated the extent of and reasons for racial disproportionality in child protective services.[28] Many poor Black neighborhoods have extremely high rates of state involvement, including child welfare investigations, family separations, and placements in foster care. In 2019, child protective services investigated one in six children in Brownsville, Brooklyn.[29] In Chicago, most child protection cases are clustered in a few almost exclusively African American zip codes.[30]

Many Black and Native American children grow up in neighborhoods with heavy state regulation of children and families while comparatively few white children do.[31] These starkly disparate neighborhood experiences are a significant component of the child welfare system's racial inequity. Racial differences in child protection investigation and foster care placement rates reflect not only children's individual chances of becoming wards of the state but also their chances of growing up in a neighborhood where state supervision of children is prevalent. This community dimension of state child protection, in turn, affects children's views of themselves, their families, their communities, and the government. The spatial concentration of child welfare agency involvement in Black neighborhoods—what I call the racial geography of child welfare—makes the child welfare system a distinct institution for Black and white children.[32]

Why haven't researchers, theorists, and practitioners focused more on the community-level impact of the child welfare system? The failure to see the child welfare system as a political institution with effects that reach beyond its individual clients stems from both philosophical and disciplinary blinders. Child maltreatment and protection are viewed as individual matters.

Historically, this was not the case. In the early twentieth century, progressive social work activists like Jane Addams conceived of their child welfare crusade as a social reform movement that addressed a range of children's problems.[33] Rescuing children from maltreatment by removing them from their homes was part of a broader campaign to remedy social ills, including poverty, that harmed children.[34] Early crusaders established pensions for widows and single mothers to reduce the need to remove their children.[35] These reformers should be faulted for judging poor immigrant families by elitist standards and excluding Black children altogether. However, they also advocated a view of child maltreatment as an urgent social problem best addressed through society-wide reforms.[36] A simultaneous but lesser-known campaign by Black club women made improving the welfare of structurally disadvantaged mothers and children a central response to racial injustice.[37]

By the 1970s, efforts to label child maltreatment as an individualized problem for dysfunctional families defeated the social vision of child welfare.[38] The government promoted, and the public accepted, a medical model of child maltreatment—harms to children as the symptom of individual parents' pathologies.[39] Instead of promoting general family welfare, child protection authorities intervene after families are already in crisis, treating parents' perceived deficits with coercive, therapeutic "cures," such as child removal, mandated counseling, and parental training classes.[40]

As advocates experimented with community-based initiatives, the federal government made clear in the Adoption and Safe Families Act of 1997 (ASFA) that state child welfare agencies should prioritize child protection over family preservation. Far from promoting social reforms, ASFA's explicit purpose is "to promote the adoption of children in foster care."[41] Congress dealt with the skyrocketing foster population not by supporting families but by speeding up family destruction.

Child welfare agencies measure their impact through individual children and families. Judges hold individual parents accountable for harms to children and apply a case-specific approach to determine the child's best interests.[42] While legal scholars frequently debate the deterrent justification for criminal punishment, they have not developed a similar analysis for the social utility of the child welfare system.[43] Policymakers do not ask whether placing more children in foster care will improve community-wide child welfare but instead claim to weigh whether placing a *particular* child in foster care makes them safer than keeping them at home.[44] Social scientists ask the same question and measure the effectiveness of child welfare policies writ large by accumulating individual children's outcomes.[45] However, they cannot fully understand the system's community-level effects by aggregating the individual effects of foster care placement.

This analysis is a by-product of sociology's romance with the manipulation of individual-level data. By leaning on these data, sociologists have sacrificed "understanding the importance of social context in human behavior."[46] Perhaps in an effort to distinguish the discipline from social work, sociologists are also seemingly less interested in studying the child welfare system as a political institution than they are in studying schools, courts, prisons, and other important institutions.[47]

Despite the recent interest in community-based practice, social work theorists nevertheless share social scientists' focus on individuals as the ultimate unit of analysis. The current norm for child welfare practice insists on outcome-based service evaluations.[48] Researchers have developed performance indicators to help caseworkers assess the impact of their interventions on the children they serve. Academics describe these "outcomes" as "advantages for clients."[49] With large datasets, evaluators analyze both individual and aggregate effects of caseworkers' interactions with families. However, this data collection bypasses the impact caseworkers have on communities.

A common response to racial disparities in the child welfare system has been implementing "culturally competent" practices to make child welfare services more sensitive to minoritized communities' distinctive needs and customs.[50] Learning cultural competence is supposed to help caseworkers deliver services more effectively to a diverse clientele and uncover biases in their views of families of color. But this strategy does not necessarily acknowledge the most significant implications of the system's racial disparities. Without addressing the system's institutional relationship to communities of color, teaching caseworkers cultural sensitivity is just as likely to help them regulate marginalized families more effectively. Social work scholars have noted that cultural sensitivity "increases client receptiveness to intervention."[51] However, this approach likely works to obscure for caseworkers, administrators, and judges the damaging community dimension of family policing interventions.

Conclusion

Intense levels of state supervision over children and families have negative consequences for family and community networks that prepare children for civic life and self-governance.[52] Caseworkers' investigations of parents often result in years of agency regulation of families, family separation, and children placed in a damaging foster system. Although promoted as necessary to protect children, family policing traumatizes children and their loved ones, infringes on rights to family autonomy, fails to provide needed material supports to families, and jeopardizes the supports that exist.[53] Child welfare policymakers should instead support ongoing efforts to dismantle the damaging family policing system and instead invest in community-building alternatives that protect children and more so than the current, coercive reliance on family investigation and separation.[54]

Researchers who have neglected the community-level impact of child welfare agencies can look to social science and legal scholarship on the community-level impact of high incarceration rates in Black neighborhoods as a model for future work.[55] Impoverished Black communities bear the brunt of the staggering increase in the prison population over the last fifty years. Research reveals that the exit and reentry of incarcerated people—like that of children in the foster system—is geographically concentrated in the poorest urban neighborhoods.[56] Incarceration has become a systematic aspect of community members' family affairs, economic prospects, political engagement, social norms, and childhood expectations for the future.[57] Literature on the community-level effects of mass incarceration provides a useful model for research on the community-level effects of child welfare agency involvement concentrated in Black neighborhoods. This research can give a more complete account of the racialized damage that family policing inflicts on communities and more reason to abolish the system.

I conducted a qualitative case study examining the impact of spatial concentration of child welfare agency involvement in a segregated Black neighborhood in Chicago with a high rate of cases in the Illinois Department of Children and Family Services (DCFS).[58] My aim was to explore how high rates of DCFS involvement affect residents' community life, social networks and civic participation, and attitudes about government and self-governance. This study expands the focus of current research from individual children to communities, from child development to civic participation, and extends social science theorizing on neighborhood effects to the child welfare system's interaction with communities.

Future research might match this study with one involving a white Chicago neighborhood where most children probably have no idea what DCFS stands for. There are no white Chicago neighborhoods with foster care placement rates like those of some Black neighborhoods.[59] It is important to understand the advantages to children of growing up without the specter of coercive state involvement in their families and communities. This is the relationship between the state and families contemplated by our constitutional democratic order and the expectation for white children in America. That is perhaps why the civil liberties attorney I spoke with was so aghast at the thought of 10 percent of all children in Washington being wards of the state—a truth we should not stand for in the case of non-white children either.

ACTION

8

Beyond Mandated Reporting
Organizing from the Inside Out

Leah Plasse and Eleni Zimiles

"I was told to be safe, not sorry—but who is staying safe?"
*"Building trusting relationships is the most important part of my work,
    and yet I'm obligated to act within a culture of suspicion."*
*"Right at a child's most vulnerable point, I'm expected to distance my-
    self, pass the buck, and remove myself."*
"I'm burnt out, I don't know what else to do."

These are a handful of the many statements from social workers and
mental health practitioners who are a part of Mandated Reporters
Against Mandated Reporting (MRAMR).[1] Mental health workers
and social service advocates work with antithetical philosophies and
mandates: to build trust and create safe spaces for families while also
policing and referring families to punitive systems. This tension leads
to impossible choices and moral binds—and causes harm to families
and practitioners.

MRAMR, an open group of social workers, counselors, and mental health providers, was created to actively address and prevent the harms of mandated reporting.[2] Mandated reporting is the obligation of professionals to report suspicions of abuse or neglect to the state. MRAMR recognizes the mandate to report as a critical part of the surveillance, criminalization, and separation of Black, Indigenous, and low-income families.[3] Our duty to report is a fundamental conflict in our field meant to support and engender trust. From firsthand experience, we have seen how mandated reporting does not keep children and families safe. Reporting is ineffective, punitive, and leads to further harm and instability.

This chapter reflects on MRAMR's origins, the work we do, and encourages others to challenge mandated reporting. We share how we collectively work to move from a social work culture of compliance and surveillance to one of consciousness, resistance, and intentional support. We outline our process, areas of impact, and share reflection questions from our perspective as cofounders of the group. We hope it will be an offering to current and future social workers and organizers. MRAMR is indebted to a legacy of impacted families and dedicated social workers who have organized steadfastly for years against the family policing system.[4] We hope to answer their call, continue their tradition, and inspire future organizing work.

Who we are

In the 2020 uprisings that followed the murder of George Floyd, individuals and communities across the United States protested the harms of state violence from police departments. Public conversation around police brutality, mass incarceration, and prison abolition became mainstream. As police departments faced increased scrutiny, social workers were often presented as an alternative to the police that could lessen the harms faced by Black and Indigenous communities. However, many in the social services field began to ask: How are we different from police? In what ways do we already police others? Are social workers an alternative to or an extension of law enforcement?

In response to the political moment, Dr. Laura Abrams, chair of UCLA Luskin's Social Welfare department, and Dr. Alan Dettlaff, former dean of University of Houston Graduate College of Social Work, released the "Open Letter to NASW and Allied Organizations on Social Work's Relationship with Law Enforcement."[5] Signed by more than one thousand social workers, the letter challenged governing bodies of the social work profession to examine their relationship with law enforcement and with the Black community. It asked social workers to consider and be accountable to the impact that years of surveillance and regulation has inflicted on Black and Indigenous families and communities.

After a member of the Faboo Listserv for New York City school social workers and counselors shared the letter, Leah put out a call for anyone interested in discussing the implications of the letter for our own practices. Eleni and several other members on the listserv showed up for the videoconference. Little did we know that we had embarked on the beginning of a much longer organizing journey. MRAMR was born.

In this first meeting we explored the ways policing extends beyond law enforcement and prisons, and how it manifests in the social work field. The Abrams and Dettlaff letter points to the racism deeply embedded in the social work profession. It pushes for the inclusion of racial justice in our ethics framework, as well as divestment from police departments and reinvestment into communities. We were moved by the demand to examine what an abolitionist politic means within social service institutions. In that spirit, mandated reporting quickly became the center of attention for our group. We recognized that mandated reporting is a pernicious requirement for all social workers across institutions and a central way the field perpetuates racism, oppression, trauma, and family separation. Mandated reporting is the gateway into family policing and other carceral systems, including foster care and the criminal justice system. Through the mechanism of reporting, social workers far too often push Black, Indigenous, and low-income families into the jaws of the family policing system.

The problem

A mandated reporter is someone who is bound by the law to report to the state any suspicion of child abuse or neglect as the law defines it. This includes mental health counselors, teachers, school officials, doctors, nurses, police, childcare workers, and a number of other professional categories. In some states, all adult residents are mandated reporters.

Social workers and counselors are required to become certified mandated reporters within their educational institutions, if not in their internship and work settings. The training includes what abuse and neglect might look like, the process of reporting, and the consequences of not making a report. It says little about what happens to a family after a report is made. Whether that is intentional is unclear, but the reality is that reporters often do not understand the process after a report is made. Once a report of suspicion is taken by the state, an investigator arrives at the family's home within twenty-four hours, often late at night, and searches the home for signs of abuse or neglect. Even if the allegation is for neglect, children can be strip-searched in an attempt to find evidence of bruising. Investigators go through and search every room in the house, open cupboards, medicine cabinets, and drawers. Investigators can show up to a young person's school and demand access to them. They can drop by the house at any time. Children may be removed while the family is under investigation. This all occurs based on *suspicion*.

These searches walk a fine line on violating Fourth Amendment rights, especially since families in most states do not have to be informed of their rights when investigators arrive. If investigators determine that abuse or neglect is present (under terms defined by the investigators), the family can be subjected to a range of punitive mandatory interventions, including required participation in drug treatment, parenting classes, or anger management courses. Families can be separated, sometimes permanently. If a parent misses the required sessions, their ability to keep their children is jeopardized. It is intrusive and punishing to parents who are being treated suspiciously, threatened with having their children taken away, and who are oftentimes unaware of their rights. It is traumatizing for young people who fear being removed from their families. Yet mandated reporter trainings do not discuss the process of investigations and the traumatic effects it has on families.

While the requirement for mandated reporter training is universal, implementation can look different across settings and states. The training often instills fear in reporters, linking any failure or refusal to report with child fatalities and the loss of our license to practice. The training pushes the narrative that mandated reporters are doing the social good of saving children from negligent caregivers, which prevents people from interrogating the mandate, their own underlying prejudices, and its harmful impact. Instead of being trained to offer compassionate care and resources that support parents and young people's autonomy, dignity, and inherent strengths, we are taught to be suspicious and report them to the authorities. The mandated reporter training is the first step in deputizing professionals to funnel families into systems of surveillance and punishment, as well as pacifying resistance against the mandate to report.

However, the training does not seem to be particularly successful. In 2022, in New York City, almost 130,000 calls were made to the state alleging suspicions of child neglect or abuse. Of those calls, 76 percent were deemed unfounded, meaning that no credible evidence was found to support the accusations. Yet, once a report is made, each family experiences the intrusive and traumatic investigations that can threaten their independence and autonomy, whether or not the evidence is ever substantiated. The impact on taxpayers is significant: $300 million is spent annually investigating allegations.[6] With 76 percent of investigations unfounded, money is being squandered because of errant and biased reporting, consuming resources that could go to programs that work to prevent the very harms that reporting seeks to find, such as universal childcare, universal health care, universal basic income, and more.

In MRAMR we invite ourselves to look honestly at the impact of our reports. What happened to the children we made calls for? How was the harm addressed? Were resources provided to meet people's needs? This invitation has demanded a reckoning for us practitioners. We often face a common reality: The outcomes are usually not effective at minimizing harm in families. Studies corroborate our lived experiences: 82 percent of families report that involvement in the family policing system made their situations significantly worse or led to no change.[7] Many of us have to work with the consequences of a report—broken trust, trauma from investigation, court proceedings, and potential family separation. We have seen the lingering impact of reports, including the unsubstantiated ones, on caregivers' records, impacting their employment opportunities and future custody cases and effectively keeping parents in poverty. Many of us have worked with families who have undergone child removals and recognize that family separation is one of the most serious traumas that we encounter in our work—and hope to help heal. Facing the consequences of our actions and the moral injury that comes from policing our clients is a fundamental part of our group's learning and accountability practices.

Since our inception, two big themes continue to surface in our monthly meetings. One is the high numbers of reports of neglect, which we came to understand as the criminalization of poverty, and the other is the racial implications of reporting given the impact of anti-Blackness at all stages of the family policing system, including reporting.

While public discourse around child safety often centers around fears of abuse, the vast majority of reports are for neglect. In New York City, 80 percent of reports are for neglect, which can include claims of a parent's failure to provide adequate food, clothing, shelter, education, or medical care.[8] There is often little to no conversation in professional spaces about how neglect is weaponized against low-income, Black, and Indigenous families, placing the burden of systemic divestment of communities onto parents and individuals.

MRAMR committed itself to addressing anti-Blackness in the family policing system. In New York City, Black children make up 23 percent of the population, yet 44 percent of investigations are imposed on Black families.[9] Across New York State, Black families are seven times more likely to be investigated than white families.[10] Even in districts with similar poverty rates, areas with higher numbers of Black residents have higher rates of investigations.[11] And once Black families are ensnared in the system, they are more likely than other families to be separated instead of being mandated services, are more likely to experience separations in general, and spend longer times in foster care. MRAMR could not look away when confronted with the systematic racist harm that mandated reporting causes.

Addressing the harm

Our discussions explore questions associated with our experiences as reporters. What alternatives exist to mandated reporting? How do we effectively describe and name the myriad and vast harms associated with reporting? How do we effectively advocate for legislative change in the mandate to report and associated policies? To this day, MRAMR seeks to answer these questions and challenges. As a group, we aim to center the experiences of impacted individuals to guide our work. We are honored to fight and organize alongside impacted families. We continue the tradition of advocacy work from the legal and social service world. We meet and collaborate with organizers from grassroots organizations, including JMACforFamilies, Movement for Family Power, *Rise* magazine, and Parents Supporting Parents. Together we read seminal works about the family policing system, such as Dorothy Roberts's *Shattered Bonds: The Color of Child Welfare* and

Torn Apart: How the Child Welfare System Destroys Black Families—And How Abolition Can Build a Safer World.[12] Our political education is paired with a commitment to building relationships with each other. As we continue to develop our political analysis, we remain grounded in firsthand experience and relationships. This foundation led us to build out our organizing internally for the group, as well as externally in our worksites and legislative avenues.

We are not the first collective of social workers organizing against the harms of the family policing system. The group sits within a long lineage of social workers forming pods and organizing to transform their practice and challenge systemic oppression. The Radical Social Work Group, in particular, provided us with the necessary groundwork in their work assessing the harms of mandated reporting and the family policing system.[13] MRAMR works to harness the expertise of our different members—people with lived experience, researchers, policy experts, parents, harm reduction specialists, former child protective services workers with insider knowledge, and network weavers. While we started with people based in New York City, social workers across the country began to join, and our group expanded to embrace a national scope.

In our meetings we brainstorm ways to be held accountable for decreasing our calls to law enforcement, generate ideas of how to organize with parents, engage in political education about the harms of family policing, and build resistance and solidarity. We have consistently seen the ways that mandated reporting impacts reporters struggling with the mandate, harms relationships with our clients and at times supervisors, but feels intractable as an institutional mechanism. Meeting after meeting, a common thread surfaced: Social workers are isolated as we wrestle with our profession's harm.

And for folks who have resisted or questioned the mandate to report, they have faced backlash or have been isolated even further. We long for community in principled struggle.

While MRAMR's focus is on the particular role of providers and their experiences at work, many practitioners have been intimately impacted by family policing. One of the ways the family policing system functions to criminalize individuals and families is to manufacture a narrative and dichotomy of *us versus them*, including *provider versus parent*. This duality holds racialized connotations as to who is knowledgeable and deserving of compassion and trust. This is steeped in the reality that a majority of social workers are white women. This duality in itself is also a white-supremacist concept. Part of our work is to explode this polarization. Many of us in MRAMR are professionals who are directly impacted by the family policing system, and MRAMR challenges narrow interpretations of who is a professional or an expert in a family's self-knowledge and well-being. By shifting the narrative of who holds power and knowledge in these relationships, we strive to cultivate autonomy for all of us.

Our structure

MRAMR's structure evolves as the group grows and changes. The format of our meetings adapts based on changing political realities, who shows up, and the fabric of our own lives and work. We work to bring in new facilitators and organizers. We've become parents, lost loved ones, changed jobs, and wrestled with the daily challenges of working in a profession harbored in crisis and urgency.

Initially, our group was predominantly made up of social workers and counselors based in New York City schools and educational settings. This provided us with common and clear targets. Yet the desire for a group like MRAMR extended beyond those of us in the field of education and New York City. Over time, the group expanded to include mandated reporters in a variety of worksites, including legal and health clinics and hospitals, and in locations across the country. When we began meeting in 2020, we were propelled by the energy and anger of the political moment. As our group has grown, we've been mindful of not duplicating the work of groups such as Repeal CAPTA or Repeal ASFA, but we are aligned with their initiatives, ready to follow their lead and mobilize to support their work.

Currently, we meet monthly and hold space for processing challenging cases and political organizing around mandated reporting. We open up the first part of the meeting for anyone seeking support and select topics and themes to discuss. In our work to challenge mandated reporting, we discuss situations where we have felt pressured to make calls, including suicidality, documentation status, homeless youth, and intimate partner violence, to name a few. We never offer "the solution." Rather, we share responses and generate ideas together.

Early on in our formation we realized we could build out structures that might deepen our collective ability to advocate against mandated reporting. We started to frame the scope of our work and where we could make an impact along three areas of oppression—internalized, interpersonal, and institutional. Our meetings became spaces to deepen our own political education, improve our problem-solving skills, and unearth the ways we've internalized the mandate to report. We hold webinar-style political-education sessions, with speakers and presenters, and in-person events. These offerings have helped us grow our connections with each other and to the work, strengthening the bonds we rely on to keep our spaces welcoming, generative, and accountable. We meet with elected officials, participate in congressional hearings, and advocate for legislation to minimize the harm of mandated reporting. This political organizing has pushed us to develop our skills in advocating for institutionalized change. At any given meeting we have a range of folks—some are new to the work, while others have been involved prior to MRAMR's creation.

Another way we built our structures was by creating a guiding set of values and norms that holds us accountable, offers a harm reduction approach, and provides us with a foundation that shapes our organizing and relationships to one another. At the core of our values is the belief that it is the *responsibility* of social workers to consider the individual within a system. We must prioritize our politicization and political consciousness-raising as social workers, a perspective we've been tasked with by the National Association of Social Workers' Code of Ethics but is so often pushed to the side.[14] When we fail to hold both the individual and the system at the same time, we are not serving our clients or our professional mandate. MRAMR takes up this task, but it is not without its challenges. This pull between a micro and macro approach is a central tension. Families will not stop being policed unless there are structural changes, and yet our MRAMR processing meetings highlight how social workers bump up against harmful structures and need support in the here and now.

Digging into our work

Over the past several years, MRAMR has been focused on political education, challenging mandated reporting policies, lowering the number of reports made, and providing safe spaces to resist mandated reporting. To continue to peel the onion of family policing professionally and personally, we often find ourselves negotiating questions and tensions across three levels: the internalized, the interpersonal, and institutional. We always keep an eye on how racism, sexism, ableism, classism, and xenophobia undergird our experiences on each level. We aim to hold up a mirror to our practices and situate our work within a more personal connection, as well as a wider political context. Our central questions remain: How do we uphold the regulation and policing of Black, Indigenous, and low-income families in our personal lives, our organizations, and our professions? What strategies can we uplift to unlearn and dismantle these practices?

Internalized: Unearthing reporting in ourselves

MRAMR operates on the principle that dismantling family policing systems necessitates introspection and a critical examination of how policing manifests within us. Failure to confront our own biases will inevitably lead us to perpetuate systematic oppression and harm. Internalization of these harmful structures can present in many forms, including racial bias, saviorism, reactivity driven by a false sense of urgency, fears of jeopardizing our professional license, moral injury, and more. In MRAMR meetings, we take time to self-reflect, recognizing that even as we advocate for systemic change and discuss organizational strategies, it's crucial to acknowledge and address how biases and personal experiences shape our individual practices in our work communities.

MRAMR believes that the journey of introspection must encompass a deep examination of our race, gender, class, and ability biases. It entails questioning the ingrained messages we've absorbed from our families, media, and educational systems regarding our roles as social workers, and grappling with how these perceptions contribute to regulation, surveillance, and harm inflicted on families. It requires us to look at how our own experiences and histories inform our beliefs about parenting and safety, and how this intersects with biases. For example, we see this in contrasting attitudes toward parental substance use. While white parents at a PTA meeting may casually mention smoking a joint without consequence, Black parents face harsh scrutiny and policing for marijuana use. Similarly, cultural perceptions shape how we view unsupervised children based on race. A white child navigating public spaces alone might be seen as independent, whereas a Black child doing the same is labeled as neglected or at risk. These disparities underscore the urgent need for us as mandated reporters to confront and dismantle the biases embedded within our practices to ensure equitable treatment for all families.

MRAMR members often discuss the pervasive, dangerous cocktail of saviorism and a manufactured sense of urgency, which ultimately manifests as forms of policing and surveillance to families. Mandated reporters are steeped in a narrative of our role as rescuers or helpers, ingrained in many through education and professional experiences. It gives social workers a false belief that our professional training and accreditation grant us superior knowledge and expertise to the person or family we are working with. Saviorism is deeply embedded in anti-Black, racialized connotations of who is the "helper" and who needs "saving." The urgency to act swiftly in the face of potential harm further compounds this paternalistic dynamic. It often translates into a default response of reactively and punitively reporting families. In our meetings we often share about the need to counter the feeling of "We have to do something!" We have to push ourselves to take the slow journey of holistic, collaborative decision-making and relationship building. This can be a challenge in nonprofit and service agencies with bloated caseloads and the high demands of the work itself, but it is a necessity. In our meetings we ask ourselves: What does it look like to pause in the face of urgency? To ask more questions and to center joint decision-making with the children and families we work with? Dispelling myths of urgency and reflecting on how our identities are tied up with being seen as a savior is critical to the work of the group.

The combination of biases, saviorism, urgency, and the fear of losing our livelihoods compels mandated reporters to police and surveil families for self-protection. We are consistently told by supervisors, coworkers, and our professional culture that it is "better to be safe than sorry," and to report any inkling of suspicions of potential harm happening in families before ensuring that all other options are exhausted. We have to ask ourselves, "For whose safety?" We have to hold the tension that the consequences of reporting are often ineffective and harmful, and that if we do not report we might lose our licenses or jobs. We are pitted against the people we are called to serve.

MRAMR members often share how we self-censor, shame, and silence our discomfort with mandated reporting. These experiences can be described as "moral injury," which is the psychological, social, and spiritual impact of betraying our beliefs and ideals. Moral injury speaks to the feelings of misalignment, shame, guilt, and powerlessness we experience when we are unable to provide care that aligns with our values of respecting people's autonomy and dignity and valuing their inherent strengths and resources.[15] Moral injury leads to burnout, maladaptive coping skills, and existential crises, and negatively impacts familial and occupational functioning.[16] When our organizations perpetuate harmful practices on families, we experience moral injury.

In our organizing work, we recognize the intertwined nature of internalized biases and institutional practices. By acknowledging and addressing biases such as paternalism and saviorism within ourselves, we create space for transformative interventions and work that aligns with our principles. Through meeting together we can stay motivated to undertake more conscientious note-taking and commit to naming and exploring ethical dilemmas and to brainstorming, investing in, and documenting creative, community-centered interventions.

We also work to clarify that not reporting is in itself an act of civil disobedience. As mandated reporters, we acknowledge our role in perpetuating harm and commit to being part of the solution by actively challenging ingrained biases and systemic injustices.

Interpersonal: Challenging reporting in relationships

The heart of many MRAMR meetings often reflects the core of social work itself—the nature of the relationships we build. We see firsthand how reporting leads to relational trauma among family members and within communities, and ruptures the trust we seek to build as social workers. Transformative change around reporting requires us to shift our on-the-ground practices, to mobilize resources effectively and creatively, and cultivate practices and procedures based in connection over punishment.

Addressing the need to shift our practicc in service of our relationships, MRAMR members created an *Alternatives to Mandated Reporting Guide*.[17] Thirsty for ways to support families outside of the family policing system, the guide offers a paradigm shift in how neglect is framed and offers reflection questions to consider preventing making a report, as well as a resource listing. By reframing neglect as a function of systems that have criminalized families living in poverty, we hope to provide mandated reporters with options to resist the family policing system. For example, families are often reported for failing to provide sufficient food. Instead of this being seen as a personal failing or bad parenting, we understand the issue as systemic. In one member's school, a community food pantry was created, and they advocated for the cafeteria to be kept open in the evening. Another member facing similar community needs called on their city officials to address wider neighborhood food insecurity. The guide speaks to how we can enter into conversations and dialogue with families in a way that honors partnership and also considers environmental context. It also can be used as a tool to guide supervision practices. The guide explores how to reframe our understanding of neglect, as well as tactics to avoid making a report and what to do when a report has to be made as a last resort, such as making a double call to a family defense advocate along with the report, ensuring family strengths are shared alongside the concerns, and calling with a family member. When neglect is reframed as systemic not personal, new creative alternatives to address people's needs emerge.

Repositioning ourselves as in relationship with families and individuals, as partners in tackling harm, as opposed to agents of policing and surveillance, opens up new possibilities to provide support outside of the harmful structures most commonly used by social workers. Community and self-determination, which are predicated on strong autonomous relationships, are critical to creating healing environments. One tool we have relied on in our group to foster this is pod-mapping, a practice in which folks outline which relationships can be resources and how these relationships can be supportive.[18] Pod-mapping is a tool that can be used with our clients seeking support outside the family policing system. We also have used it for resisting mandated reporting in our agencies.

Pod-mapping is fundamental to tailoring our interventions to uplift and highlight relationships that already exist, both in organizing and clinical work. Pod-mapping can help assess community organizations and assets and explore which types of mutual aid systems exist and which services need to be activated. Other organizations that we refer people to are also embedded in family policing. By pod-mapping we also ask for specificity, as it highlights our connections to specific staff members who might be allies and assets. Pod-mapping can be done with coworkers in our organizations, as well as with families we work with. Pod-mapping, asset-mapping, and resource mobilization extend our capacity to take care of our coworkers and clients—and hold our organizations accountable.

Focusing on the interpersonal is often where the rubber meets the road. Reflecting on our day-to-day work, we know some of the trauma that ensues after a report. On the interpersonal level, we experience the consequences of reporting culture in action. Acknowledging this harm is part of the path of transforming our practices and building wider institutional change. Understanding that all of our work is built on relationships—with the individuals and families we work with, our coworkers, with each other in MRAMR—can empower us to make changes we need to eliminate the family policing system.

Institutional: Organizing our work

Unpacking the manifestations of reporting culture inevitably leads MRAMR members toward advocacy and organizing. While collective processing, consciousness-raising, and political education is our bedrock, we've also mobilized toward cultural and policy solutions. Our experiences with reporting enlivens and deepens our advocacy work. MRAMR supports folks where they are: to engage in organizing efforts within our workplaces. We've started with conducting listening campaigns and engaging in one-on-one conversations with coworkers to better understand their perspectives and concerns on reporting. We encourage conducting organizational inventories to assess both implicit and explicit procedures related to family support and reporting: Every agency has its unique on-the-ground reporting practices. For example, some organizations have long-standing ties to community mutual aid systems or parent-support networks that are exhausted before a call. Others may use anonymous reporting more frequently or have more or less case conferencing. Our conversations have illuminated the strengths and challenges of reporting practices across settings, which informs how our strategies might change. Schools may have more long-standing relationships with caregivers than hospitals. Hotline workers have access to limited information, while inpatient treatment programs often have connection to multiple family members. Overall, we hope to promote a culture of transparency, collaboration, and accountability within our organizations.

As we build momentum internally, our group members continue to expand the work externally. Members of MRAMR take an active role across the country—from conferences, grassroots convenings, youth summits, and social work resource fairs. Members have written for scholarly and popular audiences, sharing clear political analysis grounded in experience.[19] As the conversation widens, we face the complexity of the family policing system's tendrils, which intimately entangle social work. For example, at a social work conference during an MRAMR presentation largely attended by child protective service workers concerned about over-reporting and burnout, we uncovered how social work graduate programs funnel students into employment in family policing. Finding new cross sections in justice work—in this case, of labor—deepens our conversions and organizing.

Shifting the mandated reporting training is a key part of our organizational strategy. Members were a part of the development of Columbia University School of Social Work's Mandated Supporting Curriculum, which is now provided to all social work students in the program. Similarly, K–12 school social workers collaborated to include a critical analysis in their schools' annual mandatory "child abuse and neglect" staff training.

MRAMR knows that transforming mandated reporting requires changes to both reporting laws and public service policies. Our meetings often include phone banking linked to proposed legislation connected to reporting or for community reinvestment like universal childcare. In September 2023, MRAMR members collected dozens of written testimonies from social workers for a hearing on mandated reporting hosted by the New York State Assembly's Committee on Children and Families in an effort to change reporting laws. We continue to build partnerships, delegating members to different coalition meetings and campaigns, including New York Mandated Reporting Group, Parents Legislative Action Network, and Repeal ASFA and Repeal CAPTA. We simultaneously want to support legislation that restricts or ends mandated reporting, but perhaps more importantly want to invest in antipoverty measures that are the antidote to systemic neglect. MRAMR's commitment to change mandated reporting from the inside out requires us to strategize on all levels toward a culture of care, dignity, and community-determination.

So, you're ready to organize?

Inevitably, in every meeting, a person always asks, "What can we do instead?" Not reporting is a powerful form of action and civil disobedience unto itself. Beyond that, some might say that the answer is complicated. However, in conversation after conversation, we learned it is not complicated, it is multitudinous. It requires us to focus on the internal, interpersonal, institutional, and ideological ways that we have been pressured to accept the belief that we should be surveilling and policing families. It demands that we start to organize ourselves and each other to fight for a world where families are given autonomy, dignity, and responsive care. Creating spaces to process and organize with other social workers gives us the courage to resist discriminatory reporting and invite in alternatives.

In March 2023, MRAMR held a workshop at Beyond the Bars Conference, a New York–based conference on ending mass incarceration. After an afternoon of discussing the history of mandated reporting and how specific harms of each reporting category manifested in our different work settings, we asked the inevitable question back to the group: "What do we do?" We told the group—approximately twenty-five social workers at all stages in their careers who were at various entry points to family policing—that in ten minutes we were going to come up with one hundred alternatives to reporting. Workshop participants held on to their pens and notepaper incredulously. We started the timer, and slowly the chart paper in the middle of our circle filled up—"Pay PTA members," "Set up laundry facilities in schools," "Advocate for universal childcare," "Connect to sexual abuse restorative justice circles," "Create an organizational emergency fund." When the timer went off, we had a floor covered with ideas, from the individual to the systemic. We stood in silence over the web we had woven. Poverty, violence, political stalemate, organizational bureaucracies, and more have woven a long history of tremendous, complex harm. We also saw that we have the vision and ability to nurture a relational infrastructure of care. And that we are not alone.

As reporting requirements continue to expand across the country, groups are increasingly questioning the effectiveness of mandated reporting. We are heartened by the reach of MRAMR. When new members join the group, we often hear that they have been searching for a similar space because they have wrestled with the harms of mandated reporting for so long. Mandated reporters struggle with the guilt, shame, and moral injury of being coerced to police families, but we've found that there is power and energy in being witnessed, being in conversation, and spending time to collectively strategize.

MRAMR, an in-process group, is situated within a larger abolitionist movement against family policing that is actively transforming and growing. We hope to expand the number of mental health providers and social service workers organizing to counter the harms of family policing. As we reorient and politicize our care work, we aim to bridge relationships and strategies on the individual, communal, and systemic levels, and integrate the clinical with the policy work. We hope others will seed their own groups and collaborations. We need to start where we are—where our distinct privileges and axis of power lie, where we work, where we live, and with those whom we are in relationship with. There is a social work practice beyond reporting, and we're honored to be on this long road together.

9

"I'm Not an Organizer, I Just Organized"

Amanda Wallace, Reverend Annie Chambers,

C. Hope Tolliver, Erin Miles Cloud,

and Margaret Prescod

In this chapter, we share a discussion between four different organizers with more than a century of organizing experience between them. The goal of this dialogue is not to prescribe a singular path of action, but rather to illuminate the many paths of organizing one can take to fight against the family policing system. Through this conversation, we share learnings about organizing and practical reflections, and we root ourselves in the untaught history of family policing resistance. None of us "learned" organizing from school or at our jobs, yet we are having this conversation at a time when organizer positions are moving into the nonprofit structure and academia is teaching "organizing." This is not necessarily a bad thing, but Margaret highlighted that we clarify our definition of organizer. Specifically saying,

> I worry about the distinction between the organizer and those being organized. In my work we don't make such a distinction. We don't work *for* people, but *with* them. We don't have an advocate/client relationship. We work together on the basis that our liberation is dependent on each other and also on the basis of self-help, with leadership coming from those most impacted. We share skills and work to make sure all people have the tools needed to provide leadership. I prefer to think of and call myself a "campaigner," rather than an organizer.

Throughout this piece we will use the definition of organizing that encompasses Margaret Prescod's definition of a campaigner. We invite every reader to situate themselves in this conversation with this context.

Organizing against the family policing system

Erin Miles Cloud: I'm thrilled to have this intergenerational conversation about organizing to end the child welfare system—or, as we refer to it, the family policing system. When we thought about writing this book, we really wanted to publish the work of people on the ground. I'd love it if everyone could introduce themselves and how they got started organizing against the family policing system.

Reverend Annie Chambers: I am eighty-three years old. I started organizing in the civil rights movement and the National Welfare

Rights Union. I'm also a mother. I got twenty-five children, twelve sons, and thirteen daughters, and I continued to organize even after I had my children.

Margaret Prescod: I'm an immigrant from Barbados, and when landing in the United States, our family was separated. We were homeless, as the arrangement for our housing with my grandfather fell through, and were taken in by an aunt in Brooklyn, who was active in the civil rights movement at the time. As a teenager, my sister and I spent the summer outside protesting at Downstate Medical Center in Brooklyn, where construction work was happening, but they were not hiring Black people. Seven hundred people were arrested at the site during that summer of action.[1] This was my first organizing experience in the United States.

As a young teacher in Ocean Hill–Brownsville in Brooklyn, I was trained by welfare mothers in the rights of the community to control schools.[2] I went on to cofound Black Women for Wages for Housework in 1974.[3] I later relocated to Los Angeles and, along with my sisters in the Wages for Housework Campaign, organized a meeting called Women Work and Welfare in South LA. A number of women came to that meeting who had child welfare cases and wanted to do something about it. We had known about this issue because of what was happening in Philadelphia with the Department of Human Services (DHS).[4] We started to meet with those families and founded the Department of Children and Family Services (DCFS) Give Us Back Our Children.[5]

C. Hope Tolliver: I'm a middle child of fifteen siblings. My parents moved to Chicago from the south of Mississippi. My mom needed money, and so she signed me up for a summer youth program led by a Palestinian woman doing youth organizing on the Southwest Side of Chicago. She made sure to always point out that the liberation of all people is tied to the liberation of Black people. She explained that this is why she was so focused on organizing folks on the Southwest Side of Chicago. My political entry to organizing is both through the lens of Black liberation, but also global liberation. One of my first efforts was organizing to shut down the juvenile detention center in Chicago. While doing that work, I realized that the young people who would stay late, who were the most energetic, who didn't want to leave, were also the young people who were dual systems involved (family policing and juvenile delinquency systems). These young people had family histories that were close to my own. We grew up with systems involved in our house because we were poor folks in the South Side of Chicago. The family policing system surveilled me at every juncture, including as a child, an organizer, and a mother. My own family history and my experience as an organizer made it a natural progression into my work as an abolitionist. It helped me to really think about the ways in which these systems, both mass incarceration and family policing, have historical links and are interdependent on each other insofar as they both continue a narrative of Black family dysfunctionality in order to support capitalism.

Amanda Wallace: When I think of my start in organizing, it takes me back to organizing in my own family. It was the skill of getting people together and the work of caring for children. I've always cared about the welfare of children. I had been caring for children in my own family and so naturally I went into working for the state as a child-abuse investigator. I thought that was the way to keep children safe. I quickly came to learn that the family policing system was not keeping kids safe. So, I started something new. I am very new to organizing, or at least to organizing in a political framework.

EMC: That's such a real point. So many people have been organizing their families, but we often don't see that as "organizing," even though it is very political. Can you talk more about what you mean when you say organizing from a political framework?

AW: I founded Operation Stop CPS in 2021.[6] At that time I did not have a political framework—meaning that, before that time, I wasn't thinking about being anti-capitalist or abolitionist. I wasn't explicitly connecting the work to a broader political organizing strategy for freedom or how it's an extension of colonialism and slavery. It's been a good two years of having that political grounding, and it contextualizes how deeply rooted the family policing system is in our lives.

EMC: Did you feel the impact of these systems before you had the language?

AW: Yeah, definitely, I knew it was something deeper than what I was seeing. The work was a lot of decolonizing and unlearning of the system of being a state actor.

EMC: Now, Margaret and Annie, bring us back. How many years have you been organizing?

MP: I graduated high school at sixteen, probably around 1970 or so. How many years is that?

EMC: Fifty-four years! Annie, what about you?

AC: I've been out in the movement since I was fourteen years old, so at least sixty years. Back in the civil rights movement, I was an organizer, and it continued for me up until today. I'm still an organizer.

EMC: C. Hope, what about you?

CHT: I've been organizing since I was fourteen. And that's gonna age me.

EMC: OK, I won't give the number, but I will just flag that C. Hope is the "middle-aged" organizer in our intergenerational conversation.

AC: I will tell you it's good to be my age and look back and say, "Lord, I made it." I'm gonna be a hundred, and I'm gonna tell everybody my age. I put on my stones and sparkling suits, and I'm enjoying myself. I ain't doing nothing but sitting in my house, but I look good!

MP: Right on.

EMC: So many years of organizing, and still going strong. This is what led me to this conversation, this energy and stamina, even after so much continued suffering. Can you talk about your first "awakening" to the need for organizing and how that moved you into action?

MP: All of the work was really informed by my village. I grew up on a small island, in a small impoverished rural village. The house I grew up in was an area where enslaved people lived in a type of wooden house called a chattel house (as in chattel slavery). This type of house could be picked up and moved, as we owned the house but not the land. It was without running water or electricity, it would be what people here would consider to be deep poverty, but that's really how a lot of us lived there.

It was obvious to me at the time that a lot of families were being separated because of poverty—maybe not through DCFS, but a lot of the families felt that the father or the mom had to go overseas to work to send money back to support the family. That's what my grandmother did. She left Barbados when my mother was three years old. Granma worked in a factory and cleaned houses in Brooklyn. She helped to send back money and a yearly barrel with handmade clothing and food for our family.

As a child, I was very aware of being hungry. When we were not in school, we had tea and crackers for breakfast and the next meal was dinner. I pledged to myself that no child should ever have to go hungry and that, when I grew up, I wanted to do something about that. So, after moving to the United States and graduating from university, I got a job teaching in Ocean Hill–Brownsville in Brooklyn, which at the time was a Black and Puerto Rican impoverished neighborhood with the highest school dropout rate in the country. A huge struggle at that time was for community control of schools—and mothers on welfare, who were the moms in the community, were central to that struggle. Working with them, I understood the interrelationship of sexism, racism, poverty, and family separation. They are not credited with all of their work in the movement. A lot of the men are credited, but I can tell you, I was there, and it was those mothers on welfare that carried that movement. They were also central to the movement for open admissions to the City University of New York, but none of that is ever credited to welfare mothers.[7]

I kept moving in feminist and radical spaces, and that eventually led me to a conference where I picked up material about Selma James and saw others with buttons that read "Wages for Housework."[8] This idea, "Wages for Housework," made perfect sense to me, because of the training I had in welfare rights, and also all the caregiving work of women in my village, this work kept the entire community going. I grew up watching how women's work was never done. Women were never under the tree with the fellas having a drink and playing dominoes or whatever. They were constantly working. So, I related to it. It matched what I was seeing, as I had come out of the civil rights movement and the militant Black movement, but I was seriously bothered by the sexism in the Black movement and the sectarianism of left organizations. I was still trying to find my way. Given the pledge I had made to myself as a child, and remembering the villagers I left behind in Barbados, "Wages for Housework" connected to me personally in terms of where I came from and the women that I left behind in my village.

So, along with Wilmette Brown, I cofounded Black Women for Wages for Housework.[9] One of the first campaigns we did was to win a fight in New York State for women who were on welfare to have the right to student grants at City University of New York without having their benefits cut off, as well as the university not cutting their student grant because they were on welfare. The joint student and community campaign was called "No Cuts, Just Bucks!" and was successful with the support of Assemblyman Al Vann, and in so doing established a precedent in New York State.[10]

From the beginning, we were working to get the unwaged work that caregivers were doing in their families recognized as official work. This work is contributing billions of dollars to the economy, but we were coming against the mainstream feminist movement that was equating liberation with a job outside the home. I remember, when I was teaching in Ocean Hill–Brownsville, having lunch, not with other teachers (many of whom were racist), but with the teachers' aides who were from the community, and were Black or Puerto Rican. We thought the feminists were crazy, because we knew that Black women, going back to the slave days forward, were always working outside the home and that didn't equate to liberation for us. Not only that, but for mainstream feminists to get their career outside the home, and they've got kids, they're gonna be hiring people who look like me to make it possible, to take care of your kids and family so they can go outside the home. In fact, when I was a student, I worked as a mother's helper for such a family. It is the work of welfare rights leaders like Beulah Sanders and Johnnie Tillmon and all of those saying that we have a right to be able to take care of our own kids, and we should have the money in order to do that.[11]

We were organizing for a care income and being led by mothers who relied on welfare. So, naturally that intersected our work with the family policing system. At that time, Reverend Annie knows this very well, welfare workers were coming in and taking our kids because we were poor.[12] If you look at the criteria for removing children, it's often not because of abuse but because of poverty. And as a single mother, thank goodness I was able to keep my child. Phoebe Jones and others in our women's network in Philadelphia were doing the work around child welfare and then, in LA, running into those mothers and grandmothers who were outraged because of what was happening to them, so, we began campaigning against the so-named child welfare system.

It's important to note that we were international from the start. We understood that it's really not possible to win our freedom in one particular place when most of the impoverished people in the world are not in the United States—they are in the Global South. We had to be global in our approach. We're continuing that work today with the local, national, and global work with people in the United Kingdom and India for "support, not separation" and "Give Us Back Our Children" campaigns.[13] We are working in the area of protecting and raising our children, and demanding the right to be able to do so. We are working for the right not to be forcibly sterilized. It was natural that we would be in this fight about not taking our children because we're impoverished. We focused on demanding resources and money—direct cash—to be able to take care of our children, which was very much the focus in the work we do.

EMC: It's such an honor to learn about these connections. I often think about the popularized phrase in our movement "Poverty is not neglect," and that idea is never sourced to your long and ongoing work. Thank you for pushing those connections, fighting for the direct cash assistance, and softening the ground for these ideas. For decades you have been mobilizing to connect the welfare fight and the family policing fight. So many of the answers for child safety live in the demands of the welfare mother's organizing, Black Women for Wages for Housework, Global Women's Strike, and Support Not Separation. Thank you.

Also, while I was listening to you, I was reflecting on your activism trajectory and how different it is from mine, and maybe many others who are reading this book. I spent a lot of time in nonprofit direct service work, and it informed a lot of my work now, but also has a lot of limits.

MP: By now everybody's familiar with the non-governmental organization (NGO) industrial complex. Look, I'm not opposed to anybody getting paid for the work that they do, and it's not that I'm saying, "Don't get a wage," but we do have to pay attention to how money and grants impact what we work on and how we work on it. I've seen so many movements that started out as grassroots at the base, and then what they do and how they do it gets determined by the funders. I think that's a real problem.

I suppose the movement that I was trained in was that you're working for your own liberation. You're not doing it for somebody else. I remember the late great Michael Zinzun, a former Black Panther from the Coalition Against Police Abuse—he would always say, "We will work with you, but we're not gonna work for you."[14] It's really different seeing that your own liberation is tied to this struggle, not just your advocating for someone else. You know what I mean? It's a different kind of relationship.

I suppose I came up at a time where our movement work wasn't paid. An example, my cousin Martha Prescod-Noonan, who was working in the South with the Student Nonviolent Coordinating Committee (SNCC), was paid ten dollars a week and lived with local families. The community helped take care of SNCC workers. We found other ways of surviving and really working to be anti-capitalist organizers. For twenty-two years, I was not doing waged work, I was doing full-time organizing and found ways to survive as I could. My own sanity and my own liberation are really tied to this work. I mean, it's part of what keeps me going.

Now we are getting used to organizations with big funding, and you have these expensive conferences, and people are staying at fancy hotels, and they're funded to go to the Caribbean to get some R and R, so they can continue their work in the movement. This is not the way I was trained in doing politics. It's all well and good, but I'm wondering how that impacts the work. How does it impact the relationship with the people with whom they are organizing? Of course, I know that one has to have the resources to pay rent, eat, put a roof over your head, and I am not saying folks should not get paid, but I hope that paid organizers are keeping in mind that it is the grassroots to whom they are accountable, not their funders. There is the danger that the funders determine the direction and focus of the movement. One has to keep one's eyes open.

The question for me is, are paid organizers organizing *for* other people or are they organizing *with* other people for their own liberation? How are those resources being used? Any little penny our women's network gets, our first thought is the women in the Global South. We do a lot of work on Haiti, and we are always asking, "What does the grassroots movement there need?" I was outraged to have recently found out that our women's network was the only one that we know of that sends money regularly for the movement in Haiti, despite the fact that we are largely an unfunded volunteer network. When the Karen women in Myanmar are up against the military dictatorship, and have fled to fight in the forest, we need to ask: What do they need? What practical support can be sent to them? Or to the domestic workers organizing in Lima, Peru. Or to women in Gaza facing genocide.

So, my movement work hasn't been a career. It's been—what do you call it?—it's been a path. I think it's what the ancestors have put me here to do, what they expected me to do, and I'm doing that work. I'm not putting down anybody who is getting a wage. Get it! Because we'd like to get our hands on some of that money too, particularly for the women who are most impacted in our network.

AC: You know, organizing, for me, is not a career. I tell people it's the way of life. It was my calling. You have to be able to make sure that you are willing to give. As Margaret said, no matter what you have, there's always a need for it. There's always a need to get the work done. That has been my life's work.

I've had people walk up to me and say, "Here's a hundred dollars." I maybe could have used the hundred dollars to benefit myself, but then I think, what I can do with this money that will help the movement? That comes from a lot of good training. I've met a lot of good people in my lifetime. I tell people all the time, I'm a product of Minister Malcolm X. My brother would allow me to sit in on the teachings, and it learnt me a lot because, as I've said, I've got twelve sons and thirteen daughters, and when we talk about children, people have said, "She can't raise that many children without they father!" And my father stepped in, and moved in with us, and helped me with my children. So, when people ask me how I raised my children, I said I had some of the best men in the world that helped me with my children, including my biological father. My second husband came along and helped me finish raising my children. I was twelve years old when I first got married. I've always known I had to fight to hold on to my biological children.

I saw it more and more when I went into social services. I wanted to be a social worker because I remember how the social workers used to treat me. I come from the welfare rights movement, and, let me tell you, Margaret, you are right—welfare rights women have never got the credit. We may not ever get the credit, but we know and God knows what we've done to make a difference in this world.

We are still making a difference. We have made a big difference in many movements. We have trained many people to fight. That's what the fight for welfare rights has done for me. It helped me meet up with real good women in the fight for welfare. All these people were really strong women, and they gave me strength, even though we lived in other states from each other. We would find a way to meet up, because the telephone wasn't like we have now. We'd say, "We're gonna be in New York," and I don't care what you were doing, you made your way to New York.

Like Margaret said, you got to have it in your heart. I've been doing this now for at least sixty-two years, and I never wanted to have any money. I've been offered. I live in the projects right now, but I could be in a big house that I own. That's why you hear me talk about other people that's in the movement. It's not because I have any hatred against them or anything, but you know, whenever I see them, I think about what they could have done with all that money. I want to know what they sacrificed.

EMC: I think you raise a real tension. People need money to survive. That is also in tension with the way the nonprofit industrial complex, grants, and philanthropies control and even shape the idea of organizing. I don't think anyone in this conversation believes that people shouldn't get money to live their lives, but I think what I'm hearing, and I would like to talk more about, is the anti-capitalist ethic around this work. There is a difference between the business of organizing versus organizing within a movement. Those of us who are newer to organizing are often brought into this work and trained by nonprofits and spaces with a capitalist ethic, and it becomes a journey to move away from this model.

AW: I appreciate the conversation and the grounding of their work. Just being honest, I didn't have that grounding. When I think about the men and women in my family, what has been pushed on us is getting a career. That the "American dream" is attainable if you work for it. When I got into organizing around family policing, my family was confused about what it is that I'm doing. I had a conversation with my grandmother a couple of months ago, and she said, "I really thought that you were going to have a career." So, in real time, I'm coming up against this tension, and I appreciate this conversation because it validates feelings that this is the right path for me. It's bringing up so many emotions in regard to what I've been taught versus now what I'm living in this movement.

I think what I can say now is that for people that are new to this work, you have to believe that you're on the right path to stay grounded in this work. If you are, the universe will always provide. Also, do an inventory of your cost of living in this capitalist society and all of the things that we feel like we need. While we still live in this capitalist society, we can take active steps to cut out certain things that help sustain the movement.

CHT: I'm really reflecting on this conversation, the inspiration of the generations that came before us and just the amount of knowledge that you all have. As you were speaking, I was just thinking about the ways in which movement has become very much a career. It's such a strange idea that you have to have a degree to set yourself free. How I came up, in my movement orientation, there wasn't an application to become an organizer. You were committed, you showed up, a position opened up and you filled in, and so you became a part of the work. I've seen a lot of organizer training move into universities. While there is a need to mobilize folks anywhere and everywhere, I do fear that this type of professional mobilizing has become about how many people are at an action and not how many people are coming to the meetings.

This reminds me of the conversations we were having in Chicago fifteen years ago about which young people we were centering in movement spaces. When you are looking for numbers for an action, it can be easier to center people who are "available," but that can mean overlooking young people who struggle in survival mode. There's also preference for engaging with individuals who are already motivated and primed for action. Moreover, an academic focus on "value alignment" in organizing is at odds with what it means to organize with your neighbors, with your people, and be in a real relationship. This doesn't mean that values aren't important, but rather values taught through a classroom may mean we forget that there are some people who—because of privilege—have an easier time practicing those "values." So we leave people out because they aren't "aligned," rather than working with those who could require more effort to organize with.

We, as a movement, have to make sure that we are centering the most impacted of us all. So engaging Advanced Placement students, yes! Engaging college students, yes! But also making sure that we have young people from the detention center, young people that left high school, parenting young people, the whole lot, so that the experiences, ideas, and movements are emergent and intersectional.

EMC: I think that's right. When we talk about organizing, it's often in relation to these grand concepts like freedom, liberation, et cetera. Many of us are interested in those grand concepts but become deradicalized and trained—like I was—to seek those concepts in a social justice job. It's not that people shouldn't be waged, but in a capitalist society, allowing the grandness of liberation to be captured in the capitalist labor market can actually be a way to fracture a movement and limit freedom. The social justice job or the nonprofit job does way more to normalize billionaire philanthropy than to provide new pathways for society. For most of us, these "professional organizing jobs" or "professional social justice jobs" deplete our energy and make organizing less attainable.

Amanda, your experience working in social services seems to mimic this cycle of inspiration becoming burnout. How did you go from being inside the system to building power outside of the system?

AW: In 2021, while working inside the system, I started to become aware of the harms these systems were causing, and I started to use my voice to raise my concerns and say, "I don't really feel like this is helping families." I was told to get on state committees to talk about what was happening. What I quickly saw was that it didn't really matter. They had these state committees, and they said that they were going to have people impacted by the system on these committees. Nobody impacted by the system was actually on any of these committees.

So, I started to raise my voice inside of this system, and I saw that I was a threat to the system. There was one situation in particular—I had to take custody of a child that I knew was safe. It was a moral dilemma for me because I was the person that wrote the petition for removal. My legs were the ones that walked it over to the courthouse and had the judge sign it. That child then came into custody. I was like, "What am I doing?" Yes, this is a big system and at the end of the day I did my job, but I know my action impacted this family. I quickly realized that I couldn't do this anymore. I was outraged by what was happening, but what else could I do? I just started with what made sense.

I launched Operation Stop CPS in 2021 in order to give people knowledge about the real family policing system. I'm here in North Carolina, where people still very much believe in the child *welfare* system and think it saves kids. The word *family policing* is still very new here. Families don't feel protected when they are coming forward to talk about what is happening in their lives. People still question, "Well, what did you do? Did you do all of the services that the department told you to do?" They think that there is something wrong with the parents.

Some of our strategies at Operation Stop CPS include shifting the narrative around what child welfare versus family policing is so that people have the appetite to hear what is really going on. Our political education was really trying to support communities to understand this system in a political context, to understand that family policing is the new auction block. At first when we were organizing families through Operation Stop CPS, people didn't feel safe to talk about their experiences. But as we came together, families started to feel like they could talk about what was happening to them. It was powerful, so powerful that the state started putting gag orders in place to stop them from talking. It's outrageous, and we continue to fight this.

At Operation Stop CPS, we really work to help people visualize that this is not a system that is trying to protect families. This is not a system that is trying to give people services. It is a system that is ripping families apart. I'm using my experience inside the system for ten years to validate and protect families that are coming forward about how this system has hurt them, and telling them that it's not just them. I believe it deepens the conversation when it is not just families that are impacted coming forward, but also people from inside the system saying that this system is not for anyone.

EMC: C. Hope, how did you work with young people to organize against the family policing system?

CHT: The first campaign we did was led by young people between fourteen and twenty-three who have been impacted by the family policing system. We built a base by sitting outside of some of the group homes and flyering. I was able to do some of this work because I had already been working in the detention center.

We were able to do a diversion plan with the county for young people who were supposed to go to detention centers to instead go to a youth education program. We used that program for mobilizing. We called it a youth education class, with a "field project," but really, we were mobilizing people to start talking about and thinking about the ways in which they were impacted by the family policing system.

I want to be clear that, if you are thinking about doing this, you should know that organizing is hard work. It's not just saying,

"Let's fight against the system that unjustly impacted your life," and then making a flyer. People are working through a lot of trauma that they haven't healed from or been able to talk about. Being in this journey is an important part of doing the work. Maybe you are in the court holding somebody's hand as they go through that system. Are you gonna put in the extra hours after a meeting? How will you handle listening to someone who is still processing their anger with their mother or with the system? This is what makes your question hard, Erin. The truth is that I could talk more about my campaign "wins," but I feel like I need to talk about the part of organizing that is less discussed. About the wins for individual people as they've moved through the place where they were angry, blaming, and fought their parents to a place where they see the harm of the system alongside their experiences with their family. We're talking about the ways in which systems impacted every move in their life and those systems were the thing that they were fighting against.

One of the most insidious parts of the foster care system, both in my own personal experience and in the experience of folks who have been through it, is that it's punitive, and by default that means that somebody is to blame. We had parents who were blaming their kids for not keeping whatever happened quiet, and kids who were blaming their parents for not protecting them enough. While there was a lot of language for blaming each other, nobody had the language to blame the system. People are often responding to their own trauma and abuse. In workshops, people often say someone should have intervened: I was the child waiting to be saved. I responded, "Yes, that shouldn't have happened, and someone should have protected you, but it wasn't going to be this system."

People come to movements because we have been pained by the system. That pain has real implications when organizing, and I think the best wins were being on that journey with someone and seeing them come through to the other side. It was not easy, it can be dark, but it's important work.

EMC: I love all those directions, and it gives people many different ideas for first steps into organizing. Margaret, can you all talk about different strategies and tactics you used when organizing?

MP: Our organizing operates on the basis of self-help. That's really important because that's different from the advocate-client method. We started out with meeting families going through the system, learning from and fighting cases. We've won some and we haven't won some. What we realized at a certain point is that we couldn't really keep it up, because the individual cases were relentless and the resources to fight cases were few. It is practically impossible, for example, to find lawyers willing to work on fighting cases for those who don't have the money to pay.

We realized that there was a lot of practical information that people needed. We sat down, taking the lead from families who have been through the child welfare system, and very carefully developed a "know your rights" booklet for Los Angeles County.[15] The guide shared information about what to do from the moment child welfare knocks on your door to the hearings and dealing with lawyers, and included some resources at the end. We thought it would be like a pamphlet or something like that. It's now something like twenty-three pages. It's in English and in Spanish. Families who have been through the system helped to develop questions. It's a guide for getting through this maze, and we pass it out when we table outside of family court. The guide has been very helpful for the times that we can't be there in court with people. A New Way of Life, which provides housing and services for formerly incarcerated women, including those working to reunite them with their children, have relied on this booklet.[16] We are now trying to get it available to families inside children's court.

We also did other things like press conferences and protests. The first Wednesdays in London, Philly, and LA, organizers are outside their equivalent of dependency court. We also had a series of things called "Open Children's Court," where there was a whole campaign about opening the court because the secret court stuff is a bunch of—pardon my French—bullshit, as you all know. It really hides from the public what's going on. We've done several rounds of this. We won one round in LA County, and then the social workers union sued. We also worked on legislation.

Our strategies derive from the late Johnnie Tillmon, who said we had to organize on the streets, organize to get legislation, and organize in the courts. That is very practical in a lot of ways. So we are on the streets, in the courts, and we work on legislation. In support of the work of formerly incarcerated women, we were part of winning legislation in California that poverty cannot be used to justify claims of neglect and remove children.[17] We now have to work to make sure that the system actually follows the legislation. We're also working in the area of direct cash for families. Melody Webb has a small pilot program in Washington, DC, for mothers who've been through the system, where they get a guaranteed income per month.[18]

We are growing. We used to be DCFS Give Us Back Our Children in Southern California. We now meet pretty regularly nationally as Give Us Back Our Children in a number of cities, including in Washington, DC, Philly, Cleveland, Ohio, Wisconsin, Detroit, and Baltimore. Reverend Annie knows all about it. There's a lot more I could say in terms of tactics and strategies, but those are some of the things that we're working on now, focusing on the message "take away our poverty, not our children," and for direct cash for what is now our unwaged caregiving work.

EMC: C. Hope and Amanda, what is your biggest piece of advice for organizers resisting the family policing system?

CHT: The advice I would give a new organizer is what I was given as a young organizer: "Be the person who you needed." I think that applies to so many things, from organizing, speaking to people, and just how you show up for the community. This is more definitive of who you are as an organizer than how many wins you have under your belt. I will just always believe that.

Also, I would go back to the piece around trauma. Moving through and standing ten toes deep with folks in solidarity and in kinship as they move through trauma. This is the painful part of being birthed into a movement, but it is necessary.

Last, a win in organizing is not how many campaigns or policies you've moved. It's how many people you moved. I would just say, "Stay grounded and move with people."

AW: The hardest thing for me has been the personal attacks in regard to activism—and the impact that it has had. My advice is to not go at this alone. Make sure that you have protections in place and that you work in the community. Be mindful of your own care. We're fighting for our own freedoms, and understanding that it's not a sprint, it's a marathon. Make sure that you are taking care of yourself in this fight, as well.

EMC: Margaret and Annie, in a world where movement breakdowns are so common, how have you all sustained the work and also sustained working in movement with each other for over fifty years?

MP: We've seen groups come and go. We've managed to hang in there for more than fifty years now. One way we have done that is by being accountable to each other. A lot of people don't talk about accountability and what that looks like. It is important to have a core group. That's very different from the people you see at a party, if you know what I mean. It's really important that you're starting with the people who are most impacted and to make sure that the leadership and the direction is coming from there.

I remember listening to Evo Morales, who went on to become the first Indigenous president of Bolivia, when I was in Venezuela, talking about individualism and the problem that it causes within movements. And that is absolutely true. We have really worked overtime to resist individualism and to work collectively. We have also found it important to respect autonomy. We have found, as Selma James, the founder of the Wages for Housework Campaign, says, that there is unity in autonomy. That is part of how we have survived over these fifty years, by valuing autonomy, and being accountable, and learning from each other.

For example, as the organization that I cofounded, Black Women for Wages for Housework, got more global, Indigenous women joined from the United Kingdom and India and other places. But we also had to grapple with what it meant to move from a group of Black women organizing into the category of "women of color." We are now Women of Color / Global Women's Strike, inclusive of Black, Latina, Indigenous, Asian women, and that took a lot of work. These types of struggles are not limited to the women-of-color network but are struggles we have within various autonomous organizations in our network. What it means is that if we develop a strategy or campaign as women of color that is in some way gonna fuck over the women with disabilities, or Queer Strike, or sex workers, they're gonna be saying, "Hey, wait a minute. We gotta sit down, talk about it, and work it out on the international scale." We've really been forced to have to figure out what accountability means. I'm not saying we have a blueprint for it, or that we don't mess up. It really is ongoing and daily work.

We've also been extremely careful with money, and we're accountable to each other about it. There's a difference between personal ambition and ambition for building a movement. That's a really important distinction. Money can destroy movements. We have taken a lot of care when it comes to money.

One thing I would say about day-to-day survival is that you can get tired. When I get tired, I remember the moment as a young immigrant in New York City, when my sister and I were out on a protest. We got tired and sat down on a bench. A man looked at us, and said, "Sisters, what are you all doing?" We said, "We are tired." He responded, "Sisters, get up, get on up." And we got up. That man was Malcolm X. Every time I get tired, I remember Malcolm saying, "Get on up."

EMC: That's incredible. Annie, what about you? How do we keep going?

AC: We keep going by saying the words that I say all the time. "I'm not tired yet. We keep going."

Say it: Are they tired? No! Are they tired of abusing people? No! Are they tired of killing people? No! Are they tired of starving children and not educating them? No!

So I'm not tired either. No, I'm not tired.

10

Change Everything?
Notes on Abolitionist Strategies

Erica R. Meiners

"Change everything" is the charge from the powerful scholar, mentor, organizer Ruth Wilson Gilmore.[1] Abolition involves rethinking all the structures of power that make our lives: everything.

I admit: This feels daunting.

My response to this charge is often to state what I believe: The enormity of the prison industrial complex means that there are always possibilities and places for collective engagement. Also, I remind myself that many of our demands should be common sense: decouple health care from policing, fund schools not jails! Yet when faced on the daily with this push to change everything, I can feel stuck. My everyday work is often reactive and intimate, two arenas that I find both hard and relatively easy to change.

In this political moment—another era of border-fortification, deportations, targeted criminalization of brown and Black lives, and frontal attacks on queer and trans bodies—I return to Gilmore's

148

charge as I and others wrestle with survival, strategy, and organizing. Issue- and identity-based organizing are often the frameworks forced on us by the state and violent systems—fighting reactively to challenge a component of the prison industrial complex or for trans lives in the face of an emergent and harmful policy—and these moves may provide some temporary relief. But "change everything" must also mean rethinking how we organize.

In particular, this charge is resurfacing as I think and work alongside those with decades of fierce organizing to challenge the family policing system. Why has this work been often sidelined and yet is so critical? Despite the wealth of organizing and scholarship highlighting how child welfare systems are an integral part of the prison industrial complex, abolitionist mobilizations—including my own—always seemed to struggle to prioritize the family policing system. Fighting projects such as a proposed new prison for migrants, or new punitive technologies of policing and surveillance, always emerges as urgent. Mobilizing against proposed legislation, such as attempts to criminalize co-sleeping, did not. Books challenging policing felt timely, while texts and reports highlighting resistances to the foster care system rarely surfaced on reading lists for study groups. Organizing against the family policing systems was often erased or marginalized because the campaigns and projects I am connected to are often reactive, stemming from the need to push back on threats and violence, usually from the state.

However, after decades witnessing this deprioritization, I also believe that fundamentally, family policing is also viewed as less critical, less vital, both because of lingering sentiments and mythologies surrounding children and child protection and, perhaps most potently, because those most harmed by these systems are often women, usually Black or Indigenous, and often poor. Unsurprisingly, our movements—consciously or not—can replicate facets of the same hierarchies and value systems we seek to dismantle, even when analysis about the family policing system (FPS) continues to be critical to grow an abolitionist practice!

I offer one current example of the critical importance of movements against FPS: In 2020 Governor J. B. Pritzker proclaimed the end of the juvenile prison system in Illinois: "The 150-year-old punitive model simply doesn't fulfill its mission."[2] This is a win for our organizing. Illinois, like many states, will close prisons for young people. Yet the same message that declared the end of the juvenile prison system in Illinois also announced the state's goal to create "regional residential centers" created and staffed by the Department of Juvenile Justice, purportedly to deliver more therapeutic and other services for young people.[3] (Similarly in California, a 2023 editorial headline in the *Los Angeles Times* asked the key question: "California Is Closing Its Last Youth Prisons. Will What Replaces Them Be Worse?")[4]

Parents and young people impacted by these systems ask for resources, support, care, and, yes, services—but they do not ask for a new prison or a "residential center." Even if they have pink walls or teddy bears or college programs, "kinder, gentler cages" are still prisons, as Critical Resistance co-starter Rose Braz wrote in 2006 in her public response rejecting California's proposed "gender-responsive prisons," a plan to build thirty to fifty "mini prisons" in communities across California.[5]

The analysis and tools generated by organizers working against family policing and for authentic forms of care and safety is critical, as the carceral state reforms from the juvenile prison to "regional residential centers." There is no long-haul win without this analysis, and without the people and the networks attached to challenging family policing. Movements against the FPS need abolitionist frameworks—for example, toolkits outlining actions to take instead of calling the cops—to fuel imaginative resistance strategies and to continue to make impactful changes that end these forms of violence. And projects to decarcerate and close prisons—as the closures of juvenile prisons indicates—need the analysis generated by those resisting the FPS.

Assessing how to organize differently requires a critical reassessment of my own pathway. While always leery of a list, below are some ideas and questions, all interrelated, from my learnings with others, particularly those networks working against the FPS. How to be open and grow the ability to change everything, including how we organize?

Political education: More tools and study

Since the uprising of 2020, increasingly more people identify as an abolitionist. The term also circulates in descriptions of books and convenings across a range of analytics and practices, even surfacing as a synonym for social justice. (I heard "abolition" used to describe one group's work to train school security officers to be less racist and transphobic.)

Of course, language is dynamic. And abolition is not a canonical framework, a prescriptive template, or another checklist. And I used the term before I knew exactly what it meant. But as its usage was much less widespread twenty years ago, abolition mainly had traction within organizings and groups where participation required some form of political education. When I started to think about abolition, I joined organizations and collectives. Radical community-based organizations that drive social and political movements—collectives—produce the sharpest and most useful knowledges to build the world we know we need, for the long haul. Importantly, networks, collaboratives, and collectives remind us of an important truth: No one person is the solution or the problem.

Through my participation in organizations such as Critical Resistance, I read works by W. E. B. Du Bois. I learned about a wide range of campaigns and organizing—from groups including the George Jackson Brigade and Justice NOW! I collaboratively participated in building campaigns and abolitionist projects. I read the poetry of Marilyn Buck. I joined a reading group on Dorothy Roberts's 2002 book *Shattered Bonds: The Color of Child Welfare*. These abolitionist networks supported people to both learn and unlearn a wide range of histories and knowledge bases and also demonstrated through campaigns and everydayness—however unpopular at the time—the practice of abolition. This study also demanded an analytic framework that recognizes the interconnectedness of struggle, as Audre Lorde reminded us in 1982. "There is no such thing as a single-issue struggle because we do not live single-issue lives. Malcolm knew this. Martin Luther King Jr. knew this. Our struggles are particular, but we are not alone."[6]

As someone who now has the privilege to move across multiple domains—organizing, popular or community-based education, and formal learning contexts such as schools—a disconnect between these domains is familiar. Therefore it is strange to be in this moment when everyone is an abolitionist, which should feel like a win, yet the meaning of the term is often less clear and—particularly within formal learning contexts—its ties to radical and collective grassroots organizing are often erased. Also, as we move into another era of whitelash/backlash and retaliation toward the limited gains from the uprising of 2020, quick conversions and identitarian labels will be the first to be shed. Collective practices and study, experiments that people struggle through together, these re-form bodies and ways of knowing. Perhaps practices are harder to jettison, or build into a habit, than a label is?

The start of the MAGA administration, as we scramble to support one another and to push back on hateful policies, offers me a reminder of how critical it is for campaigns and projects to deepen abolition and feminist toolkits and to produce, share, and engage in political education. We cannot do everything at once—organize on all fronts—but the analysis and organizing generated by people working against the family policing system who experiment to build safety and care are integral to any abolitionist practice, particularly as the state repeatedly co-opts our demands through reforms that do not alter the underlying carceral logics we seek to dismantle. With tools from abolition feminists, including ideas from those working against the family policing system, we are better prepared both for this moment and to continue our long-haul organizing.

Hold the wins, mourn the losses, and stay in the struggle

I claim as a win for our collective organizing that Illinois, and other states, will close the juvenile prisons. Roughly fifteen years ago, the Chicago chapter of Critical Resistance ran a scruffy abolitionist campaign called No Child Left Behind Bars. A play on the name of a dismal Bill Clinton and George W. Bush–era federal educational policy, No Child Left Behind, this campaign was aimed at raising the visibility of the long history of failed reform efforts surrounding one youth jail in Chicago, the Cook County Juvenile Temporary Detention Center, locally known as Audy Home (once the largest prison or jail for young people on the planet). Our campaign asked, "Why continue reforming this prison when we could close it down and reinvest the resources to support young people and communities?" We were a small, exuberant, and scraggly bunch. With a hustled budget of maybe a few thousand dollars, we organized political education workshops and meetings, developed materials, and held a few public events. To be generous, our events were unevenly attended.

While our campaign was likely not even on the radar of any organizations at the time, our abolitionist materials were an interruption in the status quo of mainstream criminal legal reformist organizing and service provision during that period and ignited some backlash. Some folks that operated programs in Audy Home said that our demand to close this juvenile jail/prison was a sign that we were out of touch and that this demand was unrealistic. Some folks, particularly those delivering services inside the jail/prison, felt that we were rude and creating problems.

While remnants of our work rest in a box in my closet, traces of this campaign quickly evaporated. Projects and campaigns like this one are scrubbed from any official record—and their absence from our collective memory, or their inability to achieve in their timeframe their demand, translates into failure. Too small to be important. Ineffective. Yet it is imperative to do more than shout out the names of these small initiatives that do all kinds of important labor including to seed or prefigure concepts and practices, shift culture and language, create community, support people to survive, skill up communities in new ways, and more. The National Welfare Rights

Organization and Black Women for Wages for Housework, spurred by Black feminists such as Johnnie Tillmon, pushed back on the FPS in the 1970s and named the gendering and racialization of poverty, demanded wages for the work of caring, and named the violence inherent in the state's flimsy attempts to support working poor women and families.

Yes, the losses are often so deep and shattering—how to come back after someone you love is killed by the state?—and wins are often fed to us as simply pyrrhic (may have won the battle but will lose the war). The register of calculating wins and losses, even the very concept of a win or a loss, is an economy we need to not consistently reanimate. What other registers can we inhabit that invite us to mark our labors that produce joy, freedom, and connection and that also can acknowledge and mourn the concurrent losses? What metrics and ways of remembering can also recommit all of us to collective struggle that may have no finish line?

Practice praxis

Being in community, struggle, coalition, potentially dis- or uncomfortable relations with mobilizations and configurations that are active and where learning and unlearning unfolds—these are the conditions that hold the capacity to build a stronger collective analysis and to avoid pitfalls. Or collective, messy, praxis-oriented work can hold the power to push me outside the trap of respectability politics, or liberalism. Comfort, insularity, organizing with people around identity or a "single issue"—this creates ways of knowing and working that are often too narrow and, yes, often too comfortable. In my trajectory a politics of staying with the messy and the daily is a particularly feminist praxis. And for me, learning from and working with people outside US nation-state borders continues to profoundly push me to consider what are often uncomfortable questions and move me outside of my "common sense."

While the movement to close (juvenile) prisons didn't start or end with our campaign No Child Left Behind Bars, these often intentionally extinguished organizing histories remind us to dive into the power of collective political action, experimentation, and practice, with political education, over the long haul.

As vital as highlighting the imperative of practice is paying attention to how we do that work, or how we organize, listen, and collaborate across difference. This is particularly critical, as the "we" is often, as Cathy Cohen so beautifully named in her germinal 1997 essay "Punks, Bulldaggers, and Welfare Queens."[7] We often resist and organize out of necessity because the state engineers our precarity, and we struggle to work together, even within our networks and fragile coalitions, with generosity and rigor. How do we work across difference to *not* cancel each other for our imperfection and humanness, while not replicating the harms we have experienced?

Collectivity: Ask the other question

Part of my abolitionist and feminist framework includes doing several things at the same time—for example, celebrating the wins (however short termed), focusing on the long-haul goals, and always, particularly when feeling too comfortable, trying to think with others about strategy beyond this moment, campaign, or project. Doing several things at once, and always trying to ask the other question, is possible because the "we" is never individual but instead is collective. While our actions, campaigns, projects, and more are often framed for us as divergent or unrelated—for example, exorbitant rent payments due to landlords and the threat of deportation are disconnected—our lives and our histories of radical organizing can and must remind us that people have always made these connections. For example, capitalism (landlords) depends on the subjugation of racialized groups (borders, family policing system) for its accumulation of wealth and power.

Holding multiple lenses and frameworks while organizing is hard. One tool I have found useful in urgent moments is to always try to "ask the other question." As critical race theorist Mari Matsuda wrote in 1991, a feminism that can meaningfully challenge emergent and existing forms of domination must always be flexible enough to ask the other question—or move away from our location or our struggle to notice other forms of domination and resistance. As Matsuda astutely reminds readers, "No form of subordination ever stands alone."[8] Building from Matsuda, if we are working to defund police, or to close juvenile prisons, how are we also paying attention to how other systems or forms of so-called common sense enact these same punitive practices? If our campaign challenges one facet of the prison industrial complex, such as ending mandated reporting or removing criminal records background checks for applications for employment or housing, how do our demands and tactics also challenge the underlying logics and belief systems that deepen carcerality? How do our demands and tactics not undermine how people are building and practicing freedom?

Cultivate intergenerational spaces

Yes, all movements need fresh insight and labor—this the lifeblood of organizing. I am particularly energized to follow the current radical formations in public health and social work that are rigorously taking up abolition. Yet how to move at multiple temporalities—past/present/future—and be attentive to the learnings from prior struggles and networks while also being open to new experiments and the analysis that will flow from these emergent practices? We desperately need these multiple temporalities of past/future, even when they are discordant, in our present.

Some days we are winning—often with young people in the lead. The abolitionist demands of earlier mobilizations, like Chicago's No Child Left Behind Bars, continue to reverberate—for instance, in the work led by Chicago's #NoCopAcademy organizers, who pushed to defeat a proposed $95 million police academy in Chicago, in the 2024 win to push the Chicago Public School system to divest from policing, led by young people, in the #NoCopsInCPS campaign (and in the many vibrant #FreePalestine actions through the end of 2023 into 2024). These mobilizations, indivisible from the preceding histories of struggle, are a reminder to keep our eyes on the prize. Is our goal the end of the police, or is this one critical stop on the way to building safer communities and ending systems of domination such as white supremacy and heteropatriarchy? As some jurisdictions succeed in removing uniformed police from schools, we must celebrate this win, while also continuing to organize so that others, such as social workers, do not continue the work of uniformed officers and become cops in cardigans.

Organizing against the family policing system is often, structurally, intergenerational precisely because the bodies targeted are not individuals but units, adult(s) and young people. Strategies developed by those resisting family policing are also then often intergenerational: Interrupting mandated reporting practices/laws requires adults to work with young people to safety plan to ensure both that the youth is supported and neither the young person nor the adult will interface with law enforcement. Other forms of abolitionist organizing can learn from how those within the movements against the FPS continue to mobilize intergenerational coalitions.

Thinking and moving in intergenerational networks and spaces hold the capacity to always insist on the past/future lens on the present. Yet—and perhaps my experiences are not representative—many networks struggle to maintain meaningful intergenerational participation. Adultism and ageism, and so many of the other forms of oppression we organize against, also circulate within our spheres and can effectively shut the doors to many.

◆

I certainly do not hold all the answers. I look forward to the proliferation of ideas about organizing in new ways, particularly from those with fierce histories pushing back on the FPS. We sharpen our analysis and tools, and gain imaginative fuel to change how we organize, only through collective action and associated practices of study and struggle.

11

What About Child Sexual Abuse?

C. Hope Tolliver

I often find myself facilitating workshops in rooms filled with organizers and activists. Everyone in some form recognizes the violence of mass incarceration and advocates for reform and is at least curious about abolition. The warmth of their welcome is palpable, and within this supportive environment we embark on a crucial conversation that often follows a similar path and gets stuck in a familiar, pain-filled place. I rehearse this powerful stuck place in so many organizing dialogues around abolition, and offer my practices for deep, empathetic listening to inspire others and answer this persistent question, which always seems to emerge in every workshop: What about child sexual abuse?

I start every workshop related to challenging the family policing system by talking about the war on drugs. Why? Because I know that most people can easily understand how drug war propaganda turned the crack epidemic into a prison boom and how these efforts reinforced the idea of Black criminality. The relentless portrayal of

Black people as inherently criminal led to increased criminalization, while the myth of "crack babies" painted Black mothers as dysfunctional and led to an explosion in family separation. As I speak, I see heads nod and I hear the occasional snap.

I move on to naming that mass incarceration is a legacy of slavery, perpetuating harmful stereotypes of Black men as monsters and Black women as unfit and forced to birth the next generation of enslaved people. These histories sustain the oppressive contemporary systems we seek to dismantle. The room or the audience is moving along with me, and I see people taking notes, clearly aligned with this perspective.

I then move to confront the false idea that these punitive systems produce safety, and debunk claims that police protect us from societal "monsters" and chaos. We start to discuss how the foster care system also relies on myths about protection, but in reality often shields Black children from their own families. The audience remains engaged, signaling a shared understanding, and I am hopeful that the room is moving toward understanding family policing as another state apparatus perpetuating the narrative of Black people as threats.

With this foundation, I cautiously approach the more challenging part: the call to abolish the foster care system and family policing. With this demand, the atmosphere in the room shifts. Enthusiastic snaps turn into side whispers, and the nodding heads transform into raised hands.

Anticipating the inevitable question about children who experience sexual assault and violence, I take a deep breath.

I channel compassion and firmness. As a survivor of violence, I understand the deep-rooted desire for protection and the profound disappointment when it fails to materialize. I remember what it means to sit in a room as a child and be hurt and wish for some protection. My personal connection is crucial as I frame my response.

I remind everyone that carceral systems were never designed to protect people. Government structures and punitive systems are inherently cruel and punishing, leading to further dehumanization and brutality. To genuinely protect children, we must rethink our approaches to both protection and punishment. I emphasize that the foster care system, contrary to its intended purpose, exposes children to further harm. All available research consistently demonstrates that children in foster care are more likely to experience sexual assault than are their peers outside this system. Most children are removed from their home for reasons classified as neglect, not abuse, and placing them in foster care only increases their vulnerability. The system fails to protect—it punishes. Children in foster care face higher rates of running away, teen pregnancy, self-harm, and ultimately, entry into the juvenile justice system. This experience is not one of protection but of continued harm.

I remind the room that creative solutions exist in wealthier and predominantly white communities to address child sexual harm without family separation. However, when it comes to poor children and children of color, the narrative defaults to separation, reflecting the system's belief/benefit in the inherent brokenness of our families and communities. This is a falsehood we must challenge.

Anger, hurt, and the instinct to protect ourselves often make us feel justified in responding with punishment and causing pain to those who have hurt us. However, this reaction limits our imagination and makes us reactive, rather than responsive, to the problem. While the reflexive response can feel cathartic and temporarily healing, it relies on the flawed idea that punishing an individual for harm will lead to collective change. Anger, however justified and real, obscures the potential for transformation and can stifle our compassion and our ability to envision a different, more constructive path forward. In this condition, we struggle to dream of new possibilities for healing and change, stuck instead in cycles of hurt and retaliation.

In these rooms I always acknowledge the presence of pain and hurt. Our responses to this persistent question must be rooted in compassion and an understanding that many people ask this questions from a place of personal trauma and a real desire for safer communities. We must not only answer the question itself but also make space for the underlying fears and painful experiences that shape these questions. This is slow work.

I am reminded that our movements *are* building safe, loving communities and that law enforcement and punishment are ineffective and unable to challenge violence, particularly child sexual abuse. We need solutions that foster connection, healing, and genuine protection for our children. This is our task—and this is where our focus must lie. Our compassion in our response to this question can and does spur thoughtful conversations—What does eliminate or reduce child sexual abuse?—capable of breaking down harmful and failing systems and orienting us toward building supportive and authentically protective communities.

12

Bigger Than *Roe v. Wade*

Arneta Rogers, jasmine Sankofa, Erin Miles Cloud,
Noran Elzarka, Elizabeth Ling, and Kylee Sunderlin

Reproductive justice has never just been about abortion. It's about the right to self-determination, the right to live, parent, love, have pleasure, and be free from government intrusion. Reproductive justice is the right to look ourselves in the mirror and love who we are and know that the social structures in this world reflect that love. Reproductive justice is about eradicating policing as a concept, not just when it comes to abortion, but when it comes to our bodies, our homes, and our relationships.

As feminists, we care about *Roe*. We are frustrated by decisions like *Dobbs* that undermine bodily autonomy. But our political home is not the courthouse. Our feminism is rooted in the streets, fighting for folks—queer, Black, disabled, incarcerated, and in the foster system. We have learned from the reproductive justice foremothers, abolitionists, sex workers, mothers of the welfare movement, and queer/trans activist groups such as the Santa Cruz Women Against

Rape, Combahee River Collective, and so many more, that true choice derives from our collective political power. This power will exist only when we have control of our bodies, when we eliminate all threats of state violence, and when our children and communities inherit the peaceful joy of care, not punishment.

We know then, in a post-_Roe_ world, that our organizing cannot be rooted in fear or white supremacy. Our feminism must politically _birth_ and _reproduce_ justice. This call is not about biological birth, but an inherited lineage from Black feminism that demands generation of new political life. We need to reproduce freedom lineages, create new ways of being, and politically mother each other and ourselves to justice. This means we must become more intersectional and create flexible and robust organizing strategies. This, in our opinion, starts with naming family policing as a central institution that must be confronted by reproductive justice advocates. But how do we keep pushing ourselves to be more intentional about intersectionality? Arneta Rogers, the executive director of the Center on Reproductive Rights and Justice at UC Berkeley School of Law, and coauthor of this chapter, gives us this framework to help us become more intersectional. We must ask ourselves:

1. Who is the movement currently leaving behind?
2. Who are the people who get to create and determine the structure and timing of their own families?
3. Who are the people who are supported to manage their own care _and_ can care for their own community and family outside of punitive institutions and systems?
4. Who is being shamed for their choices?
5. What do we build next?

The answers to these questions should help us figure out what we need to do, what conversations need to be had, and how to build more powerful strategies. Below we share some of our reflections on these urgent prompts.

Who is the movement currently leaving behind?

The reproductive rights movement is leaving behind the family policing movement.

The choice to parent is not just determined by access to abortion but is more centrally shaped by the community's capacity and willingness to support mothering without judgment or punishment. When we avoid integrating an understanding of the family policing system into our reproductive justice analysis, we avoid reckoning with one of the largest social welfare systems—the foster system.

In the last century, the United States has siphoned billions of dollars of public funds that could support families, to fatten the coffers of the family policing system. This has propagated an entire social services industry that is inextricably intertwined with the surveillance and policing apparatus of the foster system. In most marginalized communities, mental health services, drug treatment programs, and daycare centers are either directly funded through the family policing system or staffed by mandated reporters who must report what they believe is "bad" parenting to the family policing system. These reports trigger investigations, and when the family policing system intervenes, the state takes control of the family. The caseworker dictates every aspect of the family's daily life, inspects the food pantry, creates laundry lists of behavioral modification services that become additional parenting chores, and ultimately decides whether the family gets to legally exist. If the caseworker decides to dissolve the family, the family policing caseworker will take the children and give them to another parent that they like better, calling this adoption.

Parents deserve support. When they are wealthy, they can buy this support. Money provides nannies, vacations, large homes, reliable daycare, more individualized health care, accessible transportation, and so much more. Wealthy neighborhoods have robust schools with healthy foods, green spaces, and nonpolluted air. Rich families do not have to navigate cramped housing, rent payments, or public benefits. They can freely vent their frustrations to a high-paid therapist and seek private treatment in the most robust and supportive substance-use programs. They can have terrible moments, breakdowns, and arguments and not have the secrets of their worst moments heard by their neighbors through paper-thin walls. When poor parents are stressed, they rely on brittle social safety nets worn bare by decades of disinvestment. Their respite is often poisoned by carceral systems, coercive treatment, and "helping professionals" who talk as much to child protective services and the police as they do their clients.

We demand affirming investments in our communities that offer nonpunitive support when we inevitably struggle with one of the hardest jobs—raising a family. We need to imagine and build a world in which decisions to raise a family are not defined by criminalizing systems like family policing. The ability to raise a family free from state intrusion is fundamental to reproductive justice. We can no longer leave these mamas behind in our fight.

Who are the people who get to create and determine the structure and timing of their own families?

Adoption is not a neutral birthing choice.

When the *Dobbs* decision reversed *Roe v. Wade*, the Supreme Court proposed a "simplified" solution to forced birth—adoption. Supporters of reproductive choice were outraged that the government's *decision* to abandon women's health care would then justify the intervention of the family policing system. This should have been a revelatory moment for the reproductive rights movement. It should have been the moment these advocates joined the fight to resist the family policing system, but they didn't. How could they *still* not understand that the foster system was not about safety but control?

The inadequacy of the reproductive rights movement's response is unsurprising. For decades leading up to the *Dobbs* decision, families impacted by the family policing system and advocates argued with the reproductive rights movement to be more inclusive. Black reproductive justice scholars and activists repeatedly warned the white lawyers and their allies that exempting child services from their reproductive political frameworks would undermine the pro-choice movement. Yet these families and advocates were viewed as distracting and not strategic.

The *Dobbs* decision proved it was the white lawyers and carceral feminists who were not strategic. Both forced birth and forced family separations are offshoots of the same tree. It was inevitable that the anti-choice movement would weave them together into one cogent argument. If one is comfortable with forcing childbirth, then it stands to reason that one is fine with investigative caseworkers forcing themselves into parents' homes. If someone is okay with controlling the ways doctors provide health care, then they are likely okay with controlling the way social workers report child neglect to family policing entities. If someone is fine with the family policing system seizing a child just because the government made an intentional choice to abandon reproductive health care, then they are probably fine with the family policing system seizing a child when the government abandoned social safety nets for that family. Offering adoption as an answer to coerced birth was always on the horizon. The writing was on the wall.

We cannot ignore the structural conditions that force children into different families. While the *Dobbs* decision thrust this question to the forefront, the reproductive rights movement is not doing the necessary work to understand these intersectional fights. Perhaps for some this is a personal and difficult conversation, but when Amy Coney Barrett reversed *Roe*, she probably considered her role as an adoptive parent to sustain the anti-choice narrative. We recognize this is sensitive, calling many families into uncomfortable truths, but our goal is not shame—it is radical honesty. We cannot ignore the ways the state defines what it means to be a family. We cannot wait on the hard questions. If we do, we risk more retrenchment, more rollbacks, and less power.

Who are the people who are supported to manage their own care *and* can care for their own community and family outside of punitive institutions and systems?

Noncriminalized adults.

Reproductive rights advocates build numerous strategic fights around the law and then abandon people and movements when their demands do not fit into their legal frameworks. Parental consent is a good example. Family policing advocates have been fighting to obtain more robust protections for marginalized parents who are repeatedly confronted by an aggressive state. They are fighting against a state that wants to interrogate their children in schools, overmedicate their children in hospitals, and institutionalize their children despite their objections. They are looking to strengthen parental consent laws in situations where family police threaten the family unit. At the same time, reproductive rights advocates have also been looking into parental consent laws, often to ensure that young people can navigate their own health care choices around gender-affirming care and abortion. In a simplified manner, the family policing resisters were trying to build up the law around parental consent while the reproductive rights advocates were trying to find ways around parental consent for their young clients. So, what do we do?

There are no easy answers

First and foremost, two things can be true: Young people should be able to consent to their own gender and abortion health care, and the state should not override parental consent in order to interrogate children for family or criminal policing proceedings. The law does not always hold those complexities, but our movement can. Reproductive justice promises bodily autonomy that is free from state repression. Therefore these two positions are not in opposition but in harmony. At all points, consent laws should be about maximizing access to bodily autonomy and reducing state intervention. When we are facing state resistance, it is clear that the parent's consent should dominate, as they are the buffer protecting bodily autonomy. However, in the case of a young person accessing their own health care, such a buffer is less necessary.

As we do the hard work to figure out how to relate beyond and through laws and policies, we cannot abandon each other. We also cannot blame our people when these tensions in our laws frustrate our political ideas. We acknowledge that some parents do not want their child to have an abortion and that there are transphobic adults who harm their children. This is not acceptable, and our movements need to be committed to politically educating our people and building safety for individuals in the interim. What we can't do is permit institutions to flex moral superiority in the name of protecting people it would easily abandon. It is not acceptable for the reproductive rights movement to center white privileged bodies and abandon criminalized, poor, disabled, Black, and brown bodies under the false narrative that they are protecting the autonomy of young people.

We want a world in which families, parents, and children have the chance to work through these tensions. Young people should be able to make decisions about their health care on their own, with their parents, or with the support of another loving adult in their community. We also know that these options for young people dwindle when family policing systems overtake marginalized families. The family policing system is controlling, with rigid requirements of how the family can interact, who can be around children, and where children can go. The family policing system is designed to isolate people. It is designed to leave young people with fewer people to support their decisions. It is also a system that has historically harmed queer youth and has repeatedly been driven by conservative Christian agendas that have restricted sex education, abortion access, and many reproductive freedoms. We don't have all the answers. There will be tensions, but if we just stay siloed, we will never build the future our children deserve.

Who is being shamed for their choices?

Trans youth and criminalized parents.

A conservative parental rights movement is attacking trans youth. For example, in California, under the guise of a parental rights frame, conservative groups have tried to enact statewide forced outing policies, gender-affirming care bans, and trans athlete bans. There are no hard tensions or questions with their strategy. They are clear they want to strengthen the "right to family" to maintain evangelical, Christian, and conservative values and dominance. While the recent efforts in California have been thwarted, the nationwide threats and attacks persist.

We urgently need to have an affirmative political framework for these strategies that embodies the values of reproductive justice. This framework needs to incorporate parental rights in a capacious way that includes the right of parents to support young people in accessing and asserting their self-determination to make decisions about their bodies. We can't make short-term deals for an immediate benefit, and we will need to rely on each other to ensure we have the power to resist these shortsighted wins. Our new affirmative framework must also rethink, reorganize, and restructure the traditional ways we have thought about families, communities, and the role of the government. This new framework must radically acknowledge that if there is some sort of rift between a parent and a child, that is a normal part of relationships. State intervention makes this conflict worse, closing the space for the parent or the child to make the decisions that are best for themselves.

The specificity of this framework will not materialize in rooms saturated with privilege. We cannot spend more time centering doctors, lawyers, social workers, or the conservative right. The people most impacted must be those at the table as new affirming reproductive justice frameworks and partnerships are designed, built, and put into use. We need to build those tables together, and use each other's wisdom and resources. We know that when we root our analysis in self-determination, we will have disagreements. We are not arguing that everyone has to agree to move forward. However, these short-term conservative partnerships harm the relationships that we're building and destabilize our intimate connections across movements.

We also need to uplift and protect the models of care that exist. An example of the ingenuity of vulnerable people is the many ways young people opposing the wave of gender-affirming care bans are figuring out how to secure affirming and necessary care and services. Families that are pushed to the margins have always been forced to innovate. Our affirmative strategy must name and honor the care that exists in this very moment. It must be vigorously faithful to our ideals and our principles.

A call to action: What do we build?

The current rise in fascist tactics demands strategic action. We are furious with the rhetoric, the retrenchment, the conservative right's tactics. We also know that we are obligated to keep building, to keep reproducing freedom. To do that, we need to address our silos. We need to look back on the history of missteps. We need to call in the white feminist movement (yet again) regarding their shortsightedness. We also need to move toward an affirmative and strategic vision.

Image by Sarah Duggan at Movement for Family Power

Arneta Rogers had long been listening to the criticism of the siloing of the reproductive justice movement, and decided to build a container for a more intersectional analysis. She did not have extra time, money, or sufficient institutional support, but she knew this conversation needed to be had, and now was the time to have it. Arneta reached out to If/When/How and Movement for Family Power to convene this conversation. Together they coordinated speakers, and cultivated agendas and questions to address some of these movement gaps. It's not a silver bullet to end movement silos. Nor is it the first or last conversation of its kind. But there is an energy in this moment that is important to recognize. People are enraged with the destruction of *Roe*. Instead of falling into despair, let us use this as an opportunity to come back harder, stronger, wiser, and freer.

It is not simple. Building containers means navigating different institutional privileges. Building collective convenings means navigating internal capacity restraints, as well as intersectional identities. This conversation took multiple planning sessions and months of effort, largely spent on logistics like coordinating flights and accommodations and finding money. These are the unromantic aspects of building political power. They may not always be visible—and they are often held by the femmes and women in our movements.

The symposium in Berkeley, California, brought together nearly 150 advocates from across the country—those who see reproductive justice as their guiding framework and those who are beginning to see the deeply intertwined threads across our movements for freedom. It was an unapologetic space of reflection, hard truths, and differing perspectives. A radical acknowledgment that when systems come for our families, we must fight back, heal, and care for each other with everything we have. Not everyone needs to build a conversation on this scale, but if the resources exist, well-funded nonprofits or philanthropists should fund these strategic convenings, especially during moments of retrenchment. If the money does not exist, find a café, talk to your neighbors, start a Facebook group. The building will be different for everyone. For some, it's a reading group. Others will work to bridge the silos in policy sessions. Whatever it is, don't stop. Now is the time to build connections. We need to get bigger, better, bolder.

Let's have the hard conversations. Let's have each other's backs. Let's truly fulfill the promise of reproductive freedom to build something more dazzling, more sustainable, and more everlasting than *Roe v. Wade*.

13

Relationships, Not Reporting
The Transformative Justice Help Desk

Shira Hassan

In October 2021, I had the honor to join Interrupting Criminalization as a Transformative Justice Fellow and launch the Transformative Justice Help Desk (TJ Help Desk). Interrupting Criminalization (IC), founded and led by Andrea J. Ritchie and Mariame Kaba, supports communities that are practicing Black feminist abolitionist organizing and advocacy, serving as a movement resource hub, offering information and analysis, and creating cross-movement networks, learning, and practice spaces for organizers, practitioners, and advocates who are on the cutting edge of efforts to build a world free of criminalization, policing, punishment, and violence. As part of these offerings, the TJ Help Desk provides support to individuals and grassroots groups working to interrupt, respond to, and transform violence without the use of prisons, police, and other carceral systems.

As someone with life experience in sex work and drug use, and with several mental health diagnoses and physical disabilities, my community's practice of liberatory harm reduction (which I explain below) saved my life and the lives so many others I care about. I began organizing as a street-based teenager and then went to school, where I learned that, despite my training, I would never work as a licensed social worker, because I could not uphold the National Association of Social Workers (NASW) code of ethics and still be a part of the community that saved my life. Maintaining the boundaries required by the NASW was impossible, unimaginable.

Building on my own experiences and the practices of my communities—which have, more often than not, by choice and necessity, solved problems without police and social workers—I have, over the past three years, provided thought partnership and one-on-one consultation on transformative justice practices, tools, and frameworks through the help desk to a wide range of organizers and activists around the globe thinking through the application of transformative justice in their daily organizing and building projects that address violence without the cops and carceral systems.

Each month I support organizers working on myriad projects that interrupt violence without the use of carceral systems. TJ Help Desk callers have included activist formations and grassroots organizing groups who are working to disrupt institutional, structural, and interpersonal violence, abolitionist social workers, abolitionist social service providers, and those building community crisis response teams who seek support for noncarceral solutions, including avoiding mandatory reporting and forced hospitalization; community accountability facilitators holding restorative processes around harm and trauma; mutual aid groups caring for people who are incarcerated in prison or psychiatric facilities or who are at risk for being incarcerated or forced and coerced into hospitalization; and care teams and safety teams that form around survivors, people with disabilities, people with chronic illnesses, and psychiatric survivors.

Since the TJ Help Desk was launched in 2021, I've responded to more than seven hundred calls from close to a thousand individuals representing more than four hundred different organizations. While the majority of callers have been based in the United States, I've also fielded requests for support from the United Kingdom, Canada, Germany, Syria, Korea, Australia, South Africa, and the Philippines.

The TJ Help Desk is not an answer desk based on a "call an expert" model. Many people call about complex problems, and no one person or resource has completely figured out how to apply transformative justice principles to every situation. Rather, the TJ Help Desk offers callers an hour of time to think things through with someone who has more than thirty years' experience applying TJ values and skills in daily life and a variety of community and organizing settings. At the start of every call, I name the reality that, while there may not be an answer, this is a space where together we can metaphorically turn a crystal around and see how the light shines through from another angle. Most often, calls end with the right next question, move, or resource. The goal is to leave callers with not only concrete options but also a feeling of hope and a belief that we can break our isolation and recognize that we are all part of the solution.

This chapter focuses on one kind of call I frequently receive at the TJ Help Desk: requests for support from abolitionist organizers who work inside nonprofit structures and experience mandated reporting as crushing. The number one strategy that transformative justice relies on to interrupt violence is relationship building. Mainstream nonprofit social services simply do not allow for long-term relationship building and accompaniment, and most nonprofit social services even have policies that prevent workers from maintaining connections with people outside of the social service. Mandated reporting in particular upends nonprofit workers' abilities to build long-term relationships with the people they work with as "clients." When people seeking services know about mandated reporting, their fear of losing children, home, and family rightly prevents many people from disclosing violence, abuse, and harm or revealing any information that could lead to a report. As a result, most radical work done by abolitionist organizers in nonprofit settings must remain underground, secret. I hope by sharing some strategies for acting based on transformative justice principles in nonprofit settings, we can begin to break our isolation and take more collective action to end family policing.

Transformative justice and liberatory harm reduction help end family policing

Many abolitionists are drawn to crisis response and/or social services either because they are survivors themselves and want to be in solidarity with others who are struggling or because they hope to be able to route valuable resources away from policing and punishment and into the hands of their communities to create ecosystems of care—or both. In a world that is rife with colonialism, racial capitalism, transphobia, homophobia, and other forms of systemic violence, our communities survive using a careful alchemy of care, practice, and rebellion.

Two recent useful books, *Healing Justice Lineages: Dreaming at the Crossroads of Liberation, Collective Care, and Safety* and *Saving Our Own Lives: A Liberatory Practice of Harm Reduction*, offer historic cartographies to remind readers of the tools and strategies our people continue to use to fight back and heal.[1] Transformative justice and liberatory harm reduction are tools our ancestors, for decades, have used to transform violence without carceral systems. Both of these revolutionary methods of care focus on interrupting individual harms and transforming the root causes of systemic violence that allow harm to happen. Transformative justice and liberatory harm reduction are rooted in bodily autonomy—and view healing as inseparable from cultivating relationships and ending systemic oppression.

These terms and associated definitions can help all of us guide and design abolitionist strategies:

> **Transformative Justice (TJ)** is a political framework and approach for responding to violence, harm, and abuse. At its most basic, it seeks to respond to violence without creating more violence and/or engaging in harm reduction to lessen the violence. TJ can be thought of as a way of "making things right," getting in "right relation," or creating justice together. Transformative justice responses and interventions (1) do not rely on the state (for example, police, prisons, the criminal legal system, Immigration and Customs Enforcement, the foster care system, though some TJ responses do rely on or incorporate social services like counseling); (2) do not reinforce or perpetuate violence (such as oppressive

norms or vigilantism); and most importantly, (3) actively cultivate the things we know prevent violence (such as healing, accountability, resilience, and safety for all involved).[2]

Liberatory Harm Reduction (LHR) is a philosophy and set of empowerment-based practices that teach us how to accompany each other as we transform the root causes of harm in our lives. We put our values into action using real-life strategies to reduce the negative health, legal, and social consequences that result from criminalized and stigmatized life experiences (such as drug use, sex, the sex trade, sex work, surviving intimate partner violence, self-injury, eating disorders, and any other survival strategies deemed morally or socially unacceptable). Liberatory harm reductionists support each other and our communities without judgment, stigma, or coercion, and we do not force others to change. We envision a world without racism, capitalism, patriarchy, misogyny, ableism, transphobia, policing, surveillance, and other systems of violence. Liberatory harm reduction is true self-determination and total body autonomy.[3]

As these two frameworks demonstrate, one of the most valuable tools that abolitionist organizers have is our ability to invest in relationships. Building relationships as a violence-prevention strategy is something that offers a clear container to address violence—since all violence happens in relationships and violence can, many times, be transformed, contained, and healed within them. Investing in relationships has become a staple for many who work to end the family policing system. *Relationships, not reporting,* has become our mandate.

Many social service providers are faced with a dilemma: Most nonprofit social service employers prevent relationships from being formed through a dizzying web of rules that don't allow providers to build trust, carry a reasonable caseload that allows them to truly know their clients, or even work with people they know from their own community settings. Additionally, in many cases their jobs require them to undermine bodily autonomy and self-determination of the people they work with.

To dismantle the family policing system, we must also dismantle the nonprofit industrial complex, the prison industrial complex, and the medical industrial complex. We need to reduce the risks and impacts of "liability" regulations that put the responsibility for systemic harms on individuals and projects that are actively working to support their community's survival.

Ending family policing requires the end of mandated reporting

Many of the calls to the TJ Help Desk focused on challenging the family policing system revolve around negotiating the hurdle of mandated reporting. There are two groups of people who call the TJ Help Desk to think through mandated reporting: abolitionist organizers who are working outside mainstream nonprofits to build community-led responses to crisis and emergency, and abolitionist organizers working inside nonprofits to interrupt systemic harm and violence and divert resources back to community.

The calls from abolitionist organizers who work inside nonprofit structures struggle with the assumption and often requirement that they report to authorities. Supervisors and organizational policy exert tremendous pressure to report. Even more frustrating is the fact that most nonprofit social services have complex rules about interactions with people who seek services, created to ensure compliance with legal regimes, which prevent long-term relationship building or maintaining contact with people outside of the nonprofit setting.

Abolitionist organizers who are building noncarceral and nonpolice responses to crisis and emergency are community members developing teams and networks of people in their neighborhood or via online hubs to be a source of accompaniment for community members. Many are seeking options to embody transformative justice principles in this work through relationship building, which requires them to resist structures that undermine trust and support, including mandated reporting. Before developing a strategy around mandated reporting requirements, it is important for organizers to know the laws, which vary from state to state. Do they live in a state like Oklahoma, where every person, *even other children*, are required to report? If so, then during our TJ Help Desk call, we work to design a possible structure for the project that would allow them to navigate this extreme carceral threat.

If callers are building a program in a state where the mandated reporting laws pertain only to certain kinds of social workers, its structure can ensure that social workers are not the ones responding to calls or crises. This may help remove reporting concerns from your operating equation. Other strategies that can help your team stay in alignment with abolitionist values include: keeping some work underground, outside of organizational or institutional structures; not asking people seeking services for identification or completion of complex intake forms, so that information such as age, gender identity, or immigration status, which may trigger a reporting requirement, is not requested or shared; creating a youth-led peer response team, so young people are engaging with other young folks, which in most places does not trigger reporting requirements; and being careful with how you promote and represent your projects. Clearly defining what kinds of crises and emergencies a network can respond to may also help groups create harm reduction strategies for navigating mandated reporting laws. For example, you can create boundaries around where and when you respond to or meet with people seeking care that limit reporting requirements, such as not going into people's homes or schools.

Groups building their own crisis response teams have the flexibility to avoid certain kinds of funding support, which may place their abolitionist values at odds with grant requirements, to design a project from scratch, and to forefront the goal of minimizing adverse impacts from mandated reporting requirements while maximizing relationship- and trust-building capacities. Relationships are the most critical tool we have to interrupt violence without the use of the carceral state. Ending violence is a long-term process that requires a heavy investment of time and commitment. Investing in long-term accompaniment and relationship building is a unique gift that community-based crisis response teams must prioritize.

Providers who are survivors can be system catalysts

The vast majority of reports made to the family policing system—upward of 80 percent—are rooted in allegations of "neglect," most of which are unsubstantiated or rooted in systemic problems, including the lack of quality accessible affordable housing, health care, and education. Nevertheless, there are instances in which abolitionist social service providers who call the TJ Help Desk are aware of grave and nightmarish harm to children and families. As a survivor, I have experienced deliberate and terrifying harm, and I have witnessed it in my own work with other survivors and other young people in the sex trade and street economy. I recognize the feeling of total powerlessness when people realize that reporting to the state only leads to more violence, yet it's also the only option made available to a provider (or another "care" professional), especially because providers are made to believe that they may face threat of prosecution if they do not report. While prosecutions for failure to report have been extremely rare, many providers are frightened by reporting requirements and are regularly told they will lose their job or license or cause the agencies they work for to shut down unless they comply with mandated reporting laws.

Every month multiple abolitionist social workers and social service providers who are politicized in their practice and are looking for ways to avoid mandated reporting at all costs call the TJ Help Desk. Callers are ready to sacrifice their own professional license and jobs rather than report someone to a system that will cause further harm. The ethical dilemma for these abolitionist social service providers is not whether to report (that answer is clear—they will not). Instead, they bring different questions: How do we interrupt grave harm to children? How do we keep people safe when resources are limited? How do we connect people to resources without further putting them at risk of becoming targets of the family policing system? How do we support parents who may be intentionally isolated, either to keep the violence at home a secret or as a result of domestic violence, where a parent may be forcibly cut off from the outside world? How do we build long-term, trusting relationships inside of the nonprofit industrial complex?

When an abolitionist social service provider reaches me at the TJ Help Desk, they're often relieved to speak with someone who understands both that violent harm is happening and that they don't have to justify not using the family policing system. First, we talk through what's happening in as much detail as they can give. While not legally protected, I am committed to keeping calls to TJ Help Desk confidential so that people are able to talk through the dynamics of their workplace, as well as the dynamics of the violence they're witnessing.

Calls to the TJ Help Desk are not limited to one time only. Many times it takes us several hours over many appointments to develop possible strategies. Together, we think through all of the different things that could be done to help interrupt the violence. Is the family isolated? How can we get these folks connected to more family and neighbors? What's happening at school? Can we get as many resources into the family system as possible? Is there anyone else in this young person's life who can be their safe haven? Are the parents aware and ignoring the violence—or, if they know about the violence, would they be able to help stop it? The strategies we work to surface are ones that don't have strings attached that tie people back to systems of policing and punishment.

When people who are calling the TJ Help Desk do not need to be convinced about the harms associated with mandated reporting, we have the gift of knowing that we do not need to talk about it as an option, which gives us a freedom to think of other solutions, both simple and complex, and to consider the question of urgency. Is there an immediate harm happening that requires an immediate response or is the pressure from the state to force a report generating the wrong emergency? For example, sometimes simply not doing anything at all is the best response, albeit an uncomfortable one. Not documenting the harm may be the only available next step, and other times workers consider more radical actions to interrupt the violence, including meeting with families outside work hours and without their supervisor's knowledge.

We also have frank conversations about how these risks may impact their work and their own families. It is important that abolitionist organizers who are working in nonprofits, and who risk losing their jobs and professional license, also have a plan in place to support themselves and their loved ones. Similar to risking arrest at a direct action, where one needs to have access to legal help, bail funds, and any required medication or necessary childcare, a nonprofit worker must be prepared to lose their livelihood.

In almost every call I have with an abolitionist social service provider, there is a moment when callers blame themselves for not having the answer to the question: What will interrupt violence immediately? For many, particularly survivors, the grief of bearing witness to violence against children is unbearable. In my own journey as a survivor, self-blame has allowed a false message that I can always be in control. I internalized the message: If it's my fault or failing, then I can fix it or do this better so the violence will stop. This feeling results in the worry: If I knew how to apply transformative justice better, then I would feel more confident in my skills and be able to stop the violence I am witnessing.

We are not to blame for the violence we witness and experience. Nor can we be expected to control every situation and achieve a perfect resolution. But together, we can all be part of solutions. Young Women's Empowerment Project, an organization led by young people with current or former experience trading sex for money and who were involved in the Chicago street economy between 2002 and 2013, is one of my political homes. Being a part of a project that was led by and for young people who most of the world believed were only victims to be rescued helped teach me that, as survivors, "we are not the problem, we are the solution."[4] As we sit in the dilemma of how best to interrupt violence without policing and carceral thinking, we must also remember that, as survivors, a universe of solutions lives within us.

Breaking isolation, building abolitionist praxis

The people in the best position to support abolitionist social service providers and take down the family policing system are survivors. Abolitionist social service providers who are also survivors have lived experience either in the family policing system and/or surviving systemic violence and are therefore in an ideal position to help topple the system while addressing the immediate needs of survivors. Simply put, the best person to call and ask for help when you want to interrupt violence is another survivor. This makes survivors indispensable in the fight to end family policing.

As we fight to build communities of care outside systems of policing and punishment, including family policing, as well as a medical industrial complex that coerces medical interventions and forces disabled people into nonconsensual care, I have seen an uptick in abolitionist social service providers, particularly those with licenses, getting fired. The more visible and successful our work becomes, the greater the risk for those who are working to challenge these harmful systems.

Abolitionist organizers who are working inside nonprofit systems must reconcile the question of how to fight to dismantle a system when you are simultaneously building its capacity with your labor. For people employed by a carceral nonprofit who aim to help liberate resources and interrupt institutional violence—this is not enough. Workers inside carceral nonprofits must also organize outside their paid work to take down systems of policing, prisons, family regulation, and the nonprofit industrial complex. The sad reality is: To engage in disruption and to siphon off resources, in the short term, we can benefit from having abolitionists inside these violent systems. As someone who has never maintained employment in a social service institution but has relied on radical providers for my own care and to help my community, we need a plan for how to support those organizers who can do the work of keeping one foot firmly outside the system in order to move people from violence to liberation, from systems to safety.

Nonprofits and state systems hoard resources and treat us and our problems as their property. As we do the long-term work of toppling these systems, we need a bridge strategy. Some abolitionists are willing to work within nonprofit social services to help keep us alive until we win. Even though this is not a transformative justice approach, it is abolitionist. Our communities and loved ones need to be safer while receiving resources often available only through state or state-affiliated institutions. Without abolitionists willing to work inside social services, we would not be able to divert resources into the hands of our communities or interrupt the institutional violence people face when trying to access affirming services and goods, including hormones, abortions, or medication. Because we desperately need these resources *now*, we need ways to care for abolitionists if/when their jobs or their professional licenses are threatened. While professional licenses should never be prioritized over ending family policing and protecting families, if our organizers inside nonprofits are fired, we lose vital, creative allies who may be able to disrupt institutional violence.

We need all social workers and providers to be accountable to our abolitionist movement, but as abolitionists we need to also be accountable to abolitionists providers who are working to intervene and ultimately overturn the system from the inside, while others of us work to topple it from the outside. And as our movements work to topple these systems, we need multiple strategies. Transformative justice must happen beyond the state. We need abolitionists working to create projects and solutions that build our communities' resilience and help us rely on each other as resources. This is the purpose of the TJ Help Desk: to support people in building infrastructures and leaders that can hold us all beyond carceral systems.

By building long-term relationships, coming together in collective spaces to exchange stories, strategies, and skills, and breaking isolation, abolitionist organizers in provider roles are able to move in alignment with the larger movement to end violence. To increase resources and break the isolation experienced by abolitionist service providers, who often cannot even admit to their friends and loved ones that they do not want to use the family policing system, I started a support network through the TJ Help Desk, the Social Service Support Circle, to create and/or strengthen communities for abolitionist social workers and service providers. I did this work in collaboration with Justice Practice Collaborative, National Queer and Trans Therapists of Color Network, and Creative Interventions. The Support Circle is intended as a place where abolitionist social service workers can come together to discuss the real-life navigation of abolitionist praxis in larger nonprofit settings. We need long-lasting relationships to tear down family policing, support families being targeted, and sustain abolitionist organizers. Liberatory harm reduction and transformative justice teach us that to stay in it together we need to choose each day to fall in love with each other's survival (and survival strategies), no matter how stigmatized and criminalized.

14

Everyday People Build Extraordinary Possibilities
Parental Organizing as Key to Ending Family Policing

Shawn Koyano

Like most people, I learned in school that organizing and activism were done by brave individuals. Or people who were carefully trained. Yet as I think about the family policing system, I know the brilliance of everyday people is the backbone of resistance: BIPOC caregivers, working-poor parents, queer dads, grandmothers, and more. Out of necessity, ordinary caregivers are often at the forefront of building responses to harm and violence. These are rarely neat and polished examples full of heroic characters and happy endings. Many of these mobilizations of resistance to the family policing system are buried, too small to remember or record. I offer my own experience of organizing with other BIPOC parents to support children, faculty, and staff of color, and I focus specifically on the too familiar and horrible crisis of schools as just one attempt to thicken the record.

As Black and Asian parents, my partner and I are often faced with choices that feel impossible. When our child was ready to enter kindergarten, we initially decided to enroll them in a school outside of our neighborhood. We hoped that the access to funding and everything money brings, such as smaller class sizes, arts programs, and access to technology, would be worth the commute. We had some trepidation as the school was also located in a neighborhood with few people of color. Our fears came true. Our daughter began experiencing microaggressions and exclusion from white students. I felt deep shame realizing that we had divested from our neighborhood school to chase illusionary economic opportunities and safety at the expense of our child's social and emotional safety. We believed there was a perfect solution, or that better understanding the rules, or better foresight, or working harder would somehow result in a world where we would no longer be harmed. This magical "what if" reasoning is not real. We attempt to mitigate bad outcomes within systems designed for us not to thrive. And honing our understanding of these systems and their deep and wide impact on families, not just our own, is necessary to our collective survival.

Our time at this majority-white school was draining, and often harmful. After a trying and complicated attempt to try to organize other parents of color, our hope for continued change dwindled. Our child's school experience continued to be fraught, and my partner and I decided to enroll her in our neighborhood school, which was over 90 percent people of color, mainly Black and Asian. The school's parent organization appeared to be a close group of parents who enjoyed working together and were taking meaningful action for the school community, including supporting mutual aid initiatives for families in need, such as food bags and coat drives. When I joined, I encouraged the parent group to ask the school administration about funding, teacher hiring, and other ways the parent's group could become more involved in the school. Our suggestions were ignored or rejected by the school's administrative team with bureaucratic excuses. However, despite tensions from the administration, the parent's group continued to do work that supported the school's student and family community.

Later that school year, I received a notification from my school district that a long-term employee from our school had been charged with sexually assaulting a child while on school property. The employee had been formally charged months before the families had been notified. It is likely parents were notified only because the very next day a local newspaper included an article about the arrest. The email from the school district to parents in the school community offered resources directly from the county's prosecuting office and police department. The resources from the county law enforcement included directives such as: Do not ask your children direct questions about inappropriate touching, as this could be confusing for children; reach out to police if a child discloses anything about being inappropriately touched.

Along with that guidance, parents were offered two sexual assault hotline numbers to call for support. Parents met and discovered that a significant number of English-language learner (ELL) families and families of children with disabilities, the young people most at risk of being harmed by this staff member, had not been notified in their preferred language. I was particularly angered because I know fear and silence support an abuser's ability to abuse. We immediately notified the school administration that not all families had received the information and asked that the administration again share in accessible formats accurate and timely information with all potentially impacted families.

When violence happens in our school community, how do we respond as parents? How are we resourced to respond? The top-down approaches always seem to be individualized, yet the trauma ripples through a community. If harm happens to my child and not to another person's child, who should or can be part of the response? When the status quo we are encouraged to uphold in those situations is following law enforcement and the "expertise" of school administrators, will this actually help us? Who will help us?

Organizing as parents allowed me to lean into community care. Care for each other was reflected in our process at our meetings and events: centering the most vulnerable, offering mutual aid or resources like food or childcare, listening carefully and deeply, and ensuring there is space for all.

There is scarcity in violence and abundance in community. Systems of power, or rather those who wield (or benefit from) this power, worked overtime to extend that violence beyond school walls. We strove to not enact the same white supremacy that the school's administration deployed in their responses, which simply perpetuated harm. Yet pushing back on these systems is exhausting. When one of us needed rest and collective care, we honored this and offered as much support as we could to each other.

We gathered to discuss the best response to the news only some of us had received. There was a divide between parents who thought it important to publicly highlight the violence and others who felt the violence was something to be talked about quietly. This tension made it difficult to come to the agreement that a community gathering was even necessary, but we ultimately concluded we needed to act. Our group leaned into patience with each other. This meant that decision-making was slow and intentional. We listened to each other, even as it meant not moving quickly to respond to those in power. We were committed to each other and our purpose, and remained in practice throughout our organizing time together.

We wanted responses from the district and administration that promoted action and were also rooted in care and the needs of this community. For parents in our PTSA, our first thought was not to seek out police or even school-based social workers, but instead to support our young people and one another. Many parents also already had a distrust of social workers attached to the school system from previous negative personal experiences.

Our group of parents focused on how to care for each other as a result of the harm and how to ensure that no other families that could have been impacted were left behind. We did not all agree—I remember one parent who pushed for cameras in the building, thinking this might be a preventive measure that could ensure safety—but our shared focus was on caring for those around us. As a group, we opposed furthering any surveillance of our children. We knew the racist history of the family policing system and its specific and destructive impacts on Black and Indigenous families.

Parents immediately requested a community gathering to offer support to each family and to identify the needs of impacted families. The school's administration initially agreed, but later canceled the community meeting, day of, with no explanation. Our group gathered many resources and pleaded with the administration, recommending a coordinated community response that would outline immediate and long-term support for students and families. This would include a coordinated mental health response to support all families wondering how to talk to their children and/or provide support to students and families triggered or retraumatized from hearing about the sexual abuse at our school. We requested the ELL team be looped into this effort and make calls directly to the most likely impacted families. We recommended the response include relevant materials in multiple languages that could be shared directly with families. Our last request was that our team work collaboratively with the administration to support our community.

The response from our administrator was to direct all families back to her if they had questions and that she was coordinating with the district office to get family information translated for their next communication. Teachers sent home a one-page communication that outlined clarification on the timeline of the sexual assault, a link to a web page in English about talking to your kids about sexual assault, and previously shared hotline information with an additional telephone number for resources included. This response missed the mark.

The school didn't know how to respond with a coordinated, accessible, and culturally relevant community response. All they could offer was a pat response from law enforcement. We repeated our demand for a community meeting. We reached out to our school board representative and superintendent, and after much persistence from our parent group, pressuring top officials at the district level, parents and school leaders agreed to hold a community meeting. Top school administrators said they would do intentional outreach to families directly, with emphasis on those that had not been previously notified in their preferred language. Those in our parent group who had ties to organizers and to anti-violence activist organizations reached out to these relevant community partners to invite them to attend the meeting and to share key resources, including information on both the prevention and the impact of sexual assault for families. These outside grassroots organizations represented communities of color, and could provide accessible support in the language and culture needed by parents. Most critically, they could offer tools on how to care for children who were harmed in a supposedly safe place. None of these outside organizations centered criminal legal responses to sexual harm.

This community meeting was a fiasco, not because of the powerful presence of community-based organizations, but because people in power attempted to control the agenda. Instead of using the space for dialogue led by parents or the community-based organizations with culturally relevant experience related to sexual harm, a white person from the hospital dominated the meeting. The district had thrown a "community forum" together without listening to what we shared or understanding community needs. This white hospital representative reinforced the school district's messages that centered the power of experts and law enforcement and ignored all the labor of and ideas coming from our grassroots community responses of care. At this meeting we learned that outreach to potentially impacted families was done with only one automated phone call and an email only in English. I was furious.

The school district protected their own systems, fearful of the outcome of transparency and accountability to the impacted families. The school district wanted to keep everything quiet. As a response, we held a drop-in space for parents and caregivers to connect with those community partners to process with trained advocates and receive direct community support and care.

The details were not public knowledge, but the community felt the harm. I would run into people who would ask questions, often just rumors about the sexual abuse of a child, but the school and the district offered no response or reassurance—only silence. The school's administration ignored emails, canceled meetings at the last minute, and refused to meet. Their historic and ongoing contempt for BIPOC families exacerbated the situation, creating further havoc in the community. This all transpired at the end of the school year, and parents were left feeling confused, heartbroken, and angry.

Our PTSA refused to stay silent on the matter. We returned the following school year asking how the school would address this harm. The school's administration began to retaliate against parents they perceived as organizing. We were not allowed to meet in the school building. They worked to thwart any mutual aid efforts that had been previously implemented by the PTSA, including our food bag program for food-insecure families, our coat drives for kids, and our initiatives to strengthen language access for non-English-speaking families.

After reaching out consistently to our nonresponsive school administration, we began to reach out to teachers (including the teachers' union) and staff. During this time, teacher turnover at the school was unbelievable. More than one hundred teachers had left in seven years, far exceeding typical teacher turnover in a small elementary school. As we built relationships with current and former staff, we learned about the harm staff had endured and witnessed. Some teachers stayed quiet due to fear, while others became emboldened to share their truth, regardless of the ramifications. A few teachers aligned themselves with the school's administration for their own protection or because they believed in the same silence and tactics that keep a community divided. A culture of fear, retaliation, and silence permeated the school.

Our hurdles often felt overlapping and repetitive: layers and layers of bureaucracy, systemic erasure, ignored emails. School and district leadership that only tokenistically represented our community—or only performatively valued community. Our relationships as a collective of parents and teachers deepened and became more purposeful through our shared experience pushing back on this system.

Making change inside schools is so difficult. As parents, we are exhausted from navigating the cost of fighting against such a harmful system. Parents don't have a union. School administrations will rarely answer to us directly. Their bureaucracy does not protect us or our children. We rely on each other to be informed and to organize our response, and we hope that enough of us are able to speak up to the powers that hold our children every day. We worked to create the necessary spaces—however temporary and flawed—for parents to raise questions and to brainstorm ways to keep our children safe in a system in which we hold little institutional power.

The reality is that some of us can't attend PTSAs or school board meetings. We are often trying to survive in our homes and places of work. We are trying to figure out feeding our kids, transportation to tonight's activities, and more. As parents, sometimes it feels like a struggle just to breathe through everyday activities. Yet when faced with violence, it is clear that it is also up to us as parents to demand the end of the family policing system in our schools. We need to cultivate and rely on community-driven safety—the kind of safety that is imagined and driven by those most impacted. Safety that comes from radical care that frees us from surveillance, policing, and our ultimate destruction. People looking out for your kids not because they are in some helping profession and it's their job, but because we extend care to each other when we need it. Nestling firmly in our humanity to care for each other.

15

Movement Building and the Experiment of Movement for Family Power

Erin Miles Cloud and Lisa Sangoi

What do you do when you realize there are no systems designed to protect and nurture Black, brown, and poor families? Whether you come to this realization through your own systems involvement, by witnessing your family or friends, or political education, the question remains the same: How do you channel awareness into action? And more viscerally:

What do we do with outrage?

How do we build community care?

This book features many examples of people, groups, and organizations channeling outrage and loving on our people. We share these stories, knowing they are incomplete, because we feel compelled to emphasize building as a necessary component of abolition. While we value stories that explain the harms of this system, we are also craving things to *do*. Maybe we crave these actions because we want to be a part of change. Perhaps we want to build because we, along with our families, friends, and communities, have been impacted and have lived, for decades, without the benefit of understanding our own experiences through the prism of political education, and we cannot bear the thought of that continuing. Perhaps we are interested in the *doing* of abolition because it feels like the only way we can heal, mother/parent our children, or address the harm in our own families. Whatever the reason, we all desperately want something better, and the only way we get there is by trying.

We also believe that change requires building, and building new things is hard. It is hard when the world teaches "entrepreneurship" and "innovation" through a capitalist lens, while simultaneously underfunding and undercutting creative endeavors. It is hard when so many models of leadership are born of white supremacy. It is hard when you need to rest, mother, or be a friend or neighbor, and the structures that exist for nurturing new ideas make it nearly impossible to be in those roles and build something new. But these are also privileges, because building is not a choice for most marginalized people. It is a prerequisite to survival. If you are unhoused, you must make your shelter. If you are unbanked, you must make your own economy. The list goes on.

Lisa and Erin (we) had a choice. We *decided* to channel our outrage into building an organization. We felt that it would be helpful to the movement to abolish family policing to build Movement for Family Power (MFP), and we write this essay not to legitimize or delegitimize that choice, but to share our thought process, what we did, and some lessons learned. We hope that sharing this story increases the resources available for people to build new ideas—by giving examples of either what to do or what *not* to do.

There are also a few caveats to this essay. First, this chapter is written from the vantage point of two individuals with relative and different privileges. We have different lives, identities, and so on, but we were both mothers and women-of-color leaders in a landscape of white lawyers during a movement winter, a time in the movement's history when there is not a lot of momentum or funding.[1] There is a lot of wisdom from our shared experiences, and we aim to capture our common ground, rather than our differences. We are also writing this with a mixture of hindsight and new learning, as we are six years removed from founding the organization, but only a few months away from formally transitioning from leading it. Emotions can impact our storytelling, both clarifying lessons and potentially obscuring some truths. Our hope is to contribute to the growing collection of stories about *doing* liberation work. Every story has different versions, but this is a good place to start.

Why did we start MFP?

Movement for Family Power is a nonprofit organization that aims to put an end to the policing and punishment of families and promote a world where the dignity and integrity of all families are valued and supported.[2] MFP didn't come about because of our visionary ideas. It actually emerged due to New York City parent-led activism and the family defense movement in the early to mid-2000s.[3] We owe our existence to the care and support of reproductive justice leaders and abolitionist elders.[4]

We had good ideas and visions, but we also had privileges. We are both lawyers.[5] Lisa had a prestigious fellowship and was able to source the first grant for her salary from a former internship supervisor who was now working in philanthropy.[6] While Erin started at MFP with no pay, she could take that risk because she had a second job that provided insurance and covered her material needs. Our privileges are real and that history is relevant. When we skip these acknowledgments, we paint an inaccurate picture of what it takes to "build" something new.

MFP also owes its existence to Black pain and Black organizing. In 2017, as we were reeling from the brutal deaths of Trayvon Martin, Sandra Bland, Freddie Gray, Michael Brown, and many others, the Black Lives Matter (BLM) movement shaped our political consciousness and changed the conditions for social change.[7] We were energized by the potential of the movement and the deep organizing that preceded BLM. However, we noticed that we were among the few people in BLM organizing spaces bringing up the foster system and the family policing system as issues that needed to be addressed. We shared this concern with directly impacted activists who also wanted public outrage for the harms they experienced in the foster system, but at that time, BLM had not incorporated the family regulation system into its demands.[8] This is not a criticism of BLM, but an explanation of the political moment in 2017 that encouraged us to start MFP.

All of us have had to be called in, and every movement must continually work to deepen its intersectional analysis. This is particularly true when political and financial forces purposefully hide Black history and the stories of resistance. The truth is that most of the platformed critiques of the family policing system in 2017 were academic, legal, or policy discussions that used terms such as *dispro-portionality* and *bias* instead of *racism* and *white supremacy*.[9] Even the few convening spaces criticizing the foster system were held at places like the Ritz-Carlton in Virginia. This venue is hardly accessible to advocates doing work on the family policing system, let alone other movement organizers.

These movement silos permitted people to absorb the benevolent narrative of the family policing system, or even perceive this system as apolitical. We, and many others, were nervous about the calls to replace cops with social workers because we knew that the social work profession is infected by police logic, with mandated reporters responsible for reporting families and placing children in the foster system.[10] When we would discuss these issues with our movement friends, they would say things like, "That issue hasn't come up in our base," or "No one is organizing about it." We knew that was not true. Mariame Kaba taught us that before we come to the conclusion that no one is doing work on any given injustice, remember that someone is probably organizing around it—and that someone is probably a Black woman, and they're just not being uplifted or supported.[11] This political moment made us keenly aware that the movement to abolish family policing and its organizers needed support.

Why does MFP focus on movement building and supporting organizing?

MFP was the first abolitionist organization funded to end the family policing system and support movement building. Initially, our group, which we briefly called the National Family Defense Project, considered being a policy or legal services organization (these are also important tools for social change). However, after speaking to more than four hundred people in the child welfare ecosystem, we kept hearing, "There just needs to be a new child welfare narrative. We cannot get any laws passed or kids home, because too many people think this system keeps kids safe." After listening to this common refrain, MFP realized movement building and supporting organizers were the most pressing needs if we wanted to change the conditions for our people.[12]

Narratives change the law—and it is social movements that develop the visionary narratives that lead to sweeping policy changes.[13] This is not mere speculation, but a fact that history has taught us. It is critical that people realize that large-scale social movements fueled by grassroots organizers are *requirements* to topple massive social systems.[14] In other words, you do not get *Brown v. Board of Education* without the groundswell and movement forces that led to the Black Panthers and the civil rights movement.[15] This is not to say that laws and policies are unimportant, but rather to encourage a strategic reordering of tactics to achieve large-scale wins. We are losing cases, or seeing bad policy outcomes, not because we have not spent enough time or money on the bills but because we have not spent enough time or money on the movement.

We also knew that movements are not magical. They have critical features, such as public leaders, mass protests, organizers, creative alternative institutions, and more. These require nourishment, political education, planning, and sustained support, balanced with nimble responsiveness to changing political climates. Lisa believed that MFP could do much of this work, and Erin eagerly supported this idea. We both realized that by focusing on organizing and movements, we may be able to address silos and support real change.

Nonprofits won't save us, so why is MFP a nonprofit?

We built MFP a lot by *doing*. This is not to say we had no plans, but, with the wisdom of hindsight, we should have slowed down and talked through our visions more. On the other hand, there is something beautiful and maybe even necessary about jumping into a new idea without a huge plan. A type of combustible energy is needed to ignite a new idea. That energy gave us permission to make MFP a nonprofit.

There are many other types of formations that can and should be created: collectives, LLCs, 501(c)3s, short-term projects, campaigns, and so on. MFP is a nonprofit in part because it was the quickest way to get the funding into an account and get moving. Philanthropists give grants primarily to other nonprofits. Lisa was ending her fellowship and was running out of money. She got a grant for MFP, but there was little time to figure out how to bank this money. We quickly found a fiscal sponsor.

We deeply regret not spending more time interviewing fiscal sponsors. Fiscal sponsors are nonprofits that take you on as a project. When you sign up with them, they are supposed to manage much of your administrative work, including taxes and reporting. We had a lot of headaches with our sponsor. Under new leadership, MFP has now made a small resource discussing fiscal sponsors that we encourage everyone considering this option to read.[16]

In spite of all that, the nonprofit structure was still the best, and most efficient, way for us to meet our basic life needs and also pursue the work we envisioned. It provided a legal framework that helped us comply with Internal Revenue Service regulations, from obtaining health care to qualifying for student loan forgiveness. It also permitted us to accept charitable donations from private foundations and individual donors, as well as to pay grassroots activists for their work to fight the family policing system (in the form of charitable donations, contracts for work, material support, and more). We have never had a substantial budget, but we worked hard to break the white nonprofit mold and send resources to grassroots activists who were underpaid or not paid at all for their movement work. Over the course of our five years at MFP, we moved over at least one-third of our funds to movement partners. We are proud of this achievement, but we also believe that sharing resources should be the bare minimum function of all nonprofits that have the capacity to do so.

But, like . . . What did MFP do when you were leaders?

It's a running joke between us that the most common question MFP got was, "Well, what exactly do you all do?" When people would ask us that, our eyes would glaze over and every weary bone in our body would want to throw books against the wall. It often felt like: What didn't we do? Were the white men with "great ideas" asked this question? It didn't seem like it. The truth is we did a lot—some of it visible, some of it was discreet, and some of it was simply nonviable. However, our most important work was "ground-softening," which we hoped might bridge our efforts to the next group of leaders.

Ground-softening is a critical aspect of movements. It is work that shifts the climate to make it hospitable to large-scale social change. Students of social change understand the role of this work in building political conditions for change, even when philanthropy and "grasstop" leaders do not.[17] Ground-softening includes coalition building. A movement is not just a group of litigators, policymakers, or researchers. A movement also needs artists, healers, caretakers, rabble-rousers, and many others. Building the relationships necessary for our movement to be viable takes time and care. It also means having hard conversations that build political alignment.

We were fortunate to be invited to share space with birth workers who educated us about their fights, and who also listened to us about family policing. Many of these conversations were deep. We talked about what it means to actually come face-to-face with harm and to choose a noncarceral path. We sat in community and talked about the harm and pain within families.

Ground-softening is happening everywhere, not just at MFP. This type of work has been carried by Black femmes, queer people, and people on the margins in every movement. It is important—indeed, it is necessary—for any subsequent change, such as impact litigation, to occur. We were fortunate to collaborate with Fhatima Paulino from Ayni Institute, who has extensively studied social justice movements worldwide. We highly recommend the institute's training to anyone who wants to learn more about supporting movements. Ayni's trainings break movements down into cycles and use the framework of winter, spring, summer, and fall to provide practical ways to understand the changing needs of a movement.[18] Depending on the movement cycle, the institute also offers different interventions and ways to support movement growth. We learned from them that the ground-softening work had to be responsive to the movement's season, which in 2017 was a clear winter. Winters are tough seasons. The movement is isolated. There is scant leadership support, little tolerance for radical visions, and little or no public narrative or understanding of a particular injustice. Our mandate was to help shift that, and Ayni provided practical interventions based on the global study of movements.

Movements in their winter season need to decrease isolation around leaders, organizers, and other politically aligned movements. Here are a few ways we worked to decrease isolation and increase power:

Convenings

Our first and most significant convening we planned with the National Council for Incarcerated and Formerly Incarcerated Women and Girls.[19] This was the first cross-movement convening of organizing mothers impacted by the criminal and family policing systems. More than fifty mamas came to Philadelphia to build an analysis of the family policing system. This convening was beautiful and strategic. It decreased isolation and rapidly generated relationships, as well as new visions and analysis. We had just started MFP, and so much of the actual planning can be described only as janky, but it was one of the best activities we had worked on. From that convening emerged the first coalition of directly impacted leaders working to repeal the Adoption and Safe Families Act.[20]

Legislative campaigns

Using a legislative tool to decrease isolation in the winter of the movement has challenges and benefits. We have limited experience with this tool, but one example is the New York Informed Consent Campaign, a campaign we both agree had enormous successes and challenges.[21] We haven't come to a consensus on whether using a bill is "winter work," because there are many aspects of an isolated movement that create the perfect conditions for bills as an organizing tool. Also, there are many aspects of the winter that can make using traditional inside-game tools hazardous to the growth of the movement. However, in our experience, MFP existed in an ecosystem with incredible leaders who could carry the work in a way that deepened its impact.

Informed consent

The informed consent campaign focused on a bill that would require hospital providers to obtain informed consent before drug testing pregnant and parenting people. This bill was drafted when we came to MFP, but we wanted it to be less harmful and also believed that we could potentially use this campaign as a movement tool. Specifically, we wanted to help build a political container for cross-movement policy building in New York, change the narrative around pregnant people who use drugs, launch a wider Reimagine Support campaign to start dreaming and thinking about new ways to build safety outside the family policing system, and increase capacity and infrastructure support for BIPOC and directly impacted activism and leadership.

By working with leading policy strategists such as Eesha Pandit and Verónica Bayetti Flores of the Center for Advancing Innovative Policy, and communication experts such as Shanelle Matthews and Elizabeth Gay,[22] we were able to provide meaningful infrastructure and narrative tools to ourselves and our coalition partners. The campaign started with four organizations, but expanded to engage with approximately forty organizations in New York City. Most of these organizations had never carried a family policing bill before 2017, and now they are actively engaged in the work.

Other successes of this campaign included increasing the funding for policy and staffing capacity for New York City family policing work and resourcing more BIPOC and community leaders to head up this work. Together with campaign leaders, we built budgets; used outside pressure to push nonprofits to secure funding, write grants, and change policies; and worked with our partners to support directly impacted lead policy containers. We also experimented with nontraditional ways of crafting legislation, including art making, letter-writing campaigns, visioning sessions, and inviting musicians and poets to our meetings.

There were many problems, however, with the campaign's steering committee using a bill as a movement-building tool. First, we were not aligned with all our coalition partners on this goal, which created tension. Second, when carrying a bill, it is necessary to be responsive to the legislature, even if the intention is to build a movement. This allows people to build political power, but it can also divert energy away from movement building. It is complex, and may not be winter work. MFP left the steering committee for these reasons. On the other hand, there has been growth, but this is because other powerful leaders built that work after MFP exited. In keeping with the idea that all movement growth is interconnected, we must be clear that we deeply share the successes of this campaign with the current steering committee leaders who kept the work going when the pitfalls we mentioned revealed themselves. We can affirmatively say this experiment was a success, in part because of the vision, but mostly because of the people who carried the work after us.[23]

Growing capacity

Movement support aims to keep an eye on the capacity, needs, and infrastructure. A movement winter is characterized by unsupported leadership and diffuse infrastructure, whereas a movement spring shows signs of stable infrastructure.[24] We want to get to the "movement summer," when we are so coordinated and resourced that we can mobilize thousands of people to the street, have skilled communicators on national news, and have skilled and ethical lobbyists pushing bills, while simultaneously meeting the material needs of our people. This is possible, it has happened, but it takes extraordinarily clear vision.

As privileged individuals and a relatively privileged organization (privileged in relationship to unfunded organizers, but not in relationship to other nonprofits), we believed it was our responsibility to resource the movement by ghostwriting grants, creating social media posts, producing videos, building websites, mobilizing legal support for activists under attack, and being available to those in distress. We tried to show up whenever and wherever we were needed. While showing up is essential for the growth of a movement, it is not always quantifiable or a discrete task. Nonetheless, we believed it was the right and strategic thing to do. There has been pushback in our movement about this work. Recently, a prominent white male lawyer responded to a Black organizer in a large public event by saying that his role was only to "fight justice." He seemed to imply that his energy was better spent on the law, and he did not have the capacity to do all the things this Black organizer was asking of him. This misunderstands the organizer's message. No one should be working themselves ragged. That's ineffective. It's about all of us looking out for the growth of the movement and constantly challenging ourselves to work at our full capacity to support that movement growth, not just the growth of our own cases or legislative agenda.[25] The more we *all* support the movement's capacity, the less work it becomes for everyone, and bigger wins become more achievable.

Lawyers, and the philanthropists who fund them, need strong movements for the big legal and policy changes they seek, yet they often fail to meaningfully support movement building.[26] We hope this changes. There are many resources that explain the necessary connection between movements and the law, and it is imperative that resourced individuals learn from them and change their practices.[27]

What is MFP's impact?

In 2024, powerful organizers are becoming visible, becoming resourced, and even establishing sustainable organizations. The movement is building mutual aid networks and healing projects, and it has profoundly shifted the narrative in radical ways. MFP and many of our comrades were a part of this growth, and that's beautiful. We know we made a difference because we see the impact and because our comrades let us know that we were a part of the first wave of abolition in family policing, marching alongside them.

MFP—and all the ground-softeners who came before us and whom we worked alongside—will be a part of the big legal and policy wins that will inevitably blossom in the summer of this movement. If you are faithful to the winter work, you are seeding the ground for work to come. To depict what we write about above in a real-world example, we draw from a 2023 meeting of the New York Informed Consent Campaign. Fifty or so people and organizations, including directly impacted activists, birth workers, medical professionals, civil rights folks, and others, gathered on a call to hear from a new impact litigation attorney. He was there to get input for his litigation, which will potentially challenge the injustice of drug testing new mamas and their newborns and reporting to family policing agents. It would be a profound shift in the legal landscape if the litigation achieves its goals.

This lawyer may or may not be aware of the work required to build that informed consent coalition. He may write about it in his grant report, stating that he consulted with community groups to build "community-centered litigation." Or maybe this was just a courtesy stop in his litigation, with very little meaning to him. His understanding of his relationship to the movement or this coalition is irrelevant. What is relevant is the work of so many Black organizers and femmes that softened the ground for this litigation, who built the political container such that he can now obtain funding and input, in ways that Black women, activists, drug users, the very women this white man advocates for could not obtain. This is not an attack. No one is "coming for" this lawyer. These are facts, and this story has repeated itself throughout the history of social change. We write them more for the funders and builders who want to resource political change than to criticize the inevitable learnings of a movement.

MFP's impact is the opportunities that grow from the grounds we softened. We know this type of work, whether invisible or visible, is a part of the struggle and that MFP is a part of those wins. We know our role as clearly as we understand the ways we are connected to the people before us—the parent defense movement, the parent advocacy movement, reproductive justice leaders, and abolitionists alike. They, too, are a part of our wins and our losses. We wish we could explain the impact of MFP by doing a deep dive into all the intersecting forces that preceded us, and all that will come to be after us, but we must save that for another day. But please know, we are deeply aware that we are just one piece of the puzzle that helped reveal the next wave of anti–family policing work—and we truly coexist in an ecosystem of change.

In the next section we shift from describing MFP to what we learned from leading the organization. Take what is helpful, leave what is not, and if you ever catch us outside, we'd be happy to talk more.

Lessons learned: Some hard, some easy, some practical

The importance of vision. There is something about the ability to believe in the seemingly impossible that makes summoning the will, desire, and drive to do a thing, and then keep doing that thing, helpful. We think this is what people talk about when they talk about having vision. We had a vision—and we were in a community with activists and organizers who generously fed and believed in that vision. We feel eternally grateful for that and are super clear that to build a movement we must intentionally, relentlessly, and thoroughly support spaces for people to act on their visions.

Economy building is not just about money. Economy building is about the people you meet along the way and the friends who can bring the resources you need. It takes investing in relationships, taking chances, and building discernment around those relationships. Who are your close friends? Who is with you for the short, medium, and long term? How do you resource each other? This might mean identifying a friend with strong budgeting or graphic design skills, or someone who can cook for a community event. Building an economy requires vulnerability and trust in people. It's important to be thrilled with follow-through when it happens and not be heartbroken or defeated when it doesn't.

Organizing and nonprofit work are not the same. We spoke about the financial benefits of nonprofits at the outset, but there's a lot of value misalignment with nonprofit work. We each came into the work to support movement building, not to be an administrator, supervisor, budget consultant, human resources manager, and so on. However, these responsibilities come with nonprofit project building. Organizing also has infrastructure and administrative roles, but it's different (not easier), and there is more freedom to enter and exit organizing formations. Be clear on what you are looking for, your strengths, and the best structure for your project. Don't be like us. Take some time to really map out roles at the outset, and think about whether you want to have a fiscal sponsor (then interview potential partners rigorously), be a 501(c)3, or be a grassroots organizing group, or if you just want to get funding for a project/campaign. It can be boring and feel like it's stalling momentum, but it is critical work.

Building is not linear, and you will need to abandon projects. This is deeply experimental work, and it is super hard to say no to projects when people are under-resourced. Work with a community of folks to help you discern where your energy is best spent. Kindly communicate the "no" and the "yes" to new work and projects.

Have each other's back. You will do some things right and some things wrong. Sometimes, you may not even know what you are supposed to do and end up trying many different things. If your mistakes don't break you, then keep trying. However, if they do, take a moment and rest. If you have a supportive group of people around you, they will try to prevent your mistakes from breaking you and help you be accountable for them.

Leadership is not forever. A leader should not hesitate to take a break from leadership. The Ayni Institute teaches us that, in order to sustain our efforts and continue to push forward, we must recognize and respect our personal leadership seasons.[28] This concept has enabled us to navigate through difficult times and periods of exhaustion. At one point in our lives, we may be in a position of organizational leadership, coming up with innovative ideas and plans (a personal season of spring/summer). Then, several years later, we may shift to a more supportive role, handling operations, grant reports, and budget updates (a transition from summer to fall/winter). The key to persistence is understanding that our contributions may change over time, and that is perfectly fine.

Get comfortable with failure and disappointment. Abolitionist building is a creative process riddled with mistakes, do-overs, bursts of inspiration, and long gaps without inspiration. You will fail and be disappointed, and that's fine. It's about refinement, not getting it right.

Ask for help. This is a hard one. Black and brown femmes often struggle to receive professional support, mentorship, or investment, and must work hard to build their careers without structural support. We may expect help that never materializes and rely heavily on learned resilience. As a result, it can be difficult to overcome the effects of disinvestment and the pressure to learn by osmosis or even to fake it. These structures can ignite imposter syndrome, but one effective way to overcome this is to ask for help. Although many people who should offer help may not do so, asking for help will reveal those who are willing to assist. Finding a community of supportive individuals can make a real difference and provide a source of comfort and strength. You will find your community. That community will hold you. We promise.

Conflict may knock you out, but get back up. Every movement space is in some form of tumultuous conflict. It's a real part of liberation work. Hopefully, it changes, but we are humans, so it probably won't. We are not flattening the import of conflict—so many of us have experienced real harm, and the oppression we rage against ripples throughout the work. The heartbreak is very real, but the work must continue. When conflict happens, try to seek an elder. They can often place the conflict in perspective. Take the necessary time to heal and find the right people to support you.

Also, get back up. We don't say this to imply that anyone should take abusive punches and get back up and smile, or even bounce back from conflict within a day, month, or year. In a short space, we are trying to be transparent about the weight of conflict in our work and impart the knowledge that healing is not a destination but a journey. We also hope to normalize talking about conflict as we continue to demystify movement work, which from the outside can appear idealistic. We want to rightsize human expressions of frustration and tension, not hide from it.

Understand the difference between political relationships and friends who share our politics. When we say political relationships, we don't mean transactional relationships, but liberatory political relationships that are truly about building new futures and ideas. These political relationships are not necessarily friendships. Friends who share your politics will listen, hold you down, and, as Beyoncé says, "accept you, flaws and all." Political relationships are like neighbors. People work together to build a better community. In movement spaces, we often conflate these roles. This can be stressful and cause powerful political work to stop. So much liberatory work has stopped because of issues related more to romance and friendship, rather than political work. This is a hard lesson. We wished we had taken the time to think about what we wanted in a political relationship and how that differed from what we needed from friends who share our politics. That clarity would have breathed so much life into our movement work and helped us find understanding, true boundaries, and health.

If you say you're doing abolitionist work, then do abolitionist work. There is a dearth of resources for abolitionist work. When we get those resources, we need to do abolitionist work. We shouldn't dress reform work in abolitionist clothing or try to play mental gymnastics to justify using abolitionist credibility or money for reform work.[29] This is important from both a values standpoint and a practical one.

We believe that abolitionist work can improve the lives of Black, brown, and poor people. We also recognize that trying to do everything can overwhelm individuals and affect the clarity of the mission-driven work. It can also reduce funding available for others experimenting with abolition. However, this does not mean that abolitionists should be hostile to or cancel reformists, especially if they have also experienced the injustices we are working to change. Most of us are not born abolitionists—and the prison and punishment logics are integrated into every aspect of our lives.

Sometimes finding abolition feels like awakening to a new possibility. This is a beautiful shift, but it can also result in a type of abolitionist proselytizing that is focused more on conversion than awakening. An abolitionist organization should be committed to working on abolitionist projects, and if that balance is not maintained, it should transparently shift its mission. An abolitionist organization also has to be caring in how it relates to other theories of change. This balance between saying no to reform projects in our political work and saying yes to loving and healthy communities can be challenging, but it is important.

Save money and spend money. A lot of financial anxiety comes with spending money and fundraising, and understanding each other's perspectives on saving and spending is tricky. If you have the privilege of having cash reserves, do it. However, not spending enough money can lead to overtaxing yourself and doing work that you're not skilled at. It's important to have someone with financial expertise outside your organization regularly review your budget and assess this balance.

Accept and discern feedback. When starting an organization, it is imperative to find ways to gather feedback, whether it's through an advisory committee, listening sessions, or surveys—but mostly through real relationships, because, let's face it, leaders are hardheaded and the culture of feedback can be tricky.

Additionally, it's important to discern the weight of competing feedback. A good example is the question we raised above, "What does MFP do?" The weight of this question truly depended on who was asking. Some people didn't believe/understand movement building, so answering the question required us to explain our work. Others asked us this question because they were trying to help us become clearer and more steadfast in our vision or saw us drifting away from our mission. Still others asked,

"What does MFP do?" in the midst of conflict and tension. In those moments the question, in part, reflected the strained relationships and not always the value of the work. It can sometimes be hard to discern and properly weigh feedback. This is why having support is so important.

It is also true that incorporating feedback may not happen immediately. When resources are scant and capacity is low, it can be easy to say, "Well, that's a great point, but we can never do that." If something is not possible at that moment, a better approach is to save that feedback in a list or share it with your board so that you can revisit the idea when conditions shift.

Share resources. MFP shared a lot. We shared grant language, social media posts, graphics, research, relationships with grasstops, and more, with others in the movement. We removed our brand and encouraged others to rebrand tools as their own. Why? Because we don't want the movement to waste time recreating resources. We also benefited from colleagues who did the same. The Possible LAB is a project that collates and collects organization resources, for example.[30] They offer sample grant language libraries, budget templates, and other invaluable tools. We also have deep gratitude for people like Kassandra Frederique, who connected us with operation specialists, grant funding, and research support. The number of people who shared their work with us is truly too long for this book, but we are infinitely grateful.

Effort versus work, and the importance of joy. A close friend of Erin's once said that if someone invited you to stand in a room with forty rubber balls being rapidly thrown at you, you'd likely decline, but if someone invited you to play dodgeball, you'd probably consider it. The world looks really different when we invite people into play-ful effort rather than work. She said this during a time when Erin was finding it particularly hard to lead. This friend was not trying to sugarcoat her struggles. Still, she was pushing Erin to find different ways of understanding her relationship to work and to help her build healthier and more sustainable habits.

For many of us, the idea of struggling for freedom means con-stant work, and maybe there is some shame when it doesn't feel "hard" or that we are living a "soft life." Maybe the root of this feeling comes from existing in a sea of chaos and needing to be the sibling who held it together. Or maybe the root cause is our desire to honor the incredible sacrifices of our parents by matching their efforts. For some people, this urgent energy results from surviving in a world that refuses to be kind. Whatever the reason, we all live in a world that rewards "work" over play, even though play and creation take enormous effort, talent, and skill.

Erin's friend was offering feedback. She knew that liberation needed everyone at their maximum potential for the longest period of time possible. To have that type of longevity, we needed to seri-ously reevaluate where we learned how to work and consider other ways to understand effort that aren't rooted in trauma or capitalism. It's not a simple lesson to integrate, but it actually seems super clear when we look back. MFP needed way more silliness and play, and we especially needed it when joy felt most elusive.

So, what's next? After all this, are you lying flat on your couch and ready to give up?

We would be lying if we didn't say that the last five years weren't the hardest professional and personal years of our lives. In hindsight, starting an organization right before the Covid-19 pandemic and the 2020 uprisings, while raising small children, was possibly some of the dumbest shit we ever did, but it was also really beautiful. MFP was a part of a moment transforming our understanding from "child welfare" to "family policing," during a time when many of us were actively experimenting with abolition. Would we trade the winter movement work to be energized in the spring? Probably. But you don't get to pick your movement season, and supporting movement building means truly being accountable to what the movement needs from you—not what you want it to need.

To that end, we have both been radically honest that neither of us should be in leadership right now. We moved through our summers of leadership, and we know we need time to restore, learn, and re-energize. When we realized this, we considered the possibility of sunsetting MFP. We ultimately decided against this, because, although we were depleted, MFP is still very viable as a structure. MFP is coming into its own identity, and the organizational purpose and role are solidifying. We are utterly amazed at jasmine Sankofa's leadership, and we are thrilled to watch her and our movement comrades thrive in the spring of the work.

As for us, we didn't give up. We changed. Stopping feels like a privilege we cannot afford. People have been through a lot and sacrificed so much, yet they keep going. We also continue to be outraged. As we write this chapter, and finish one more cycle of movement effort, we are once again pondering:

What do we do with outrage?

How do we build community care?

When we build work for liberation and situate ourselves in the action of abolition, we should revisit these questions repeatedly.

In 2024, we have noticeably less energy, and considerably more wisdom and community. We know we need some time to learn. We also know we need to rest and not be in charge of anything. That has nothing to do with giving up. Giving up is abandoning the vision for a new world. Giving up is *not* leaving a nonprofit, stepping down from a leadership role, or even taking a yearlong nap on the floor.

So we keep going. When we started to ask our community what we should do, they told us to take care of our people. We are mothers as much as we are daughters, and some significant changes in our families have reminded us that we are not promised to each other forever. We need to tend to our children, our people, and ourselves. This, too, is movement building.

In community (and in winter hibernation),
Lisa and Erin

Acknowledgments

We are because of the communities that love and sustain us with fresh bread, beloved time, generative and principled dissent, payday loans, childcare and fur-family support, car rides, love, proofreading, campaign strategizing, jokes, feedback, critical engagement, hugs, and so much more. This project would not be possible without our intertwined and individual networks, and we share so much gratitude for their love, labor, generosity, and brilliance, which are threaded throughout this project.

A number of groups and mobilizations supported and shaped this project from the start, including Accountable Communities Consortium, Beyond the Bars, Black on Both Sides, Black Women for Wages for Housework, Critical Resistance, Illinois Black Advocacy Initiative, Just Beginnings Collaborative, Mandatory Reporting Is Not Neutral Project, Mandatory Reporters Against Mandatory Reporting, DHS Give Us Back Our Children, Operation Stop CPS, If/When/How, Movement for Family Power, and National Council for Incarcerated and Formerly Incarcerated Women and Girls. This book is possible because of our collective vision and labor.

We would also like to thank the following people who offered key labor and insight at crucial moments: Alexis Neely, Anthony Arnove, DeAnn Alcantara Thompson, Jasmine Wali, Laura Chow

Reeve, Maria Isabelle Carlos, Mathilda de Dios, Sam Kirk, and Shawn Koyano.

Finally, to some of our people who watched us at computers when we could have been hanging out with you—Charlie Cloud, Adam Cloud, and Nora Cloud; to those who taught us to be thinkers and fighters—Michael Tanksley, ShaunMoses Tolliver, Amiya C. Tolliver, Ahmad C. Tolliver, and Antonia Clifford; to the people who remind us what it is to be cared for, seen and loved unconditionally—Danny Hanson, Kathe Perez, Paul Darby, and Laurien Rouxlyn Galindo Moore; and to the people who remind us that an army of lovers can never lose, including Laurie, Leslie, Mollie, and Nic.

Appendix

Our creativity is an essential tool in our organizing to end family policing. To that end, we have included a visual appendix of just some of the tools and campaigns created by communities working to end family policing.

Excerpts from *You Matter: An Illustrated Guide for Young People Beyond Mandatory Reporting*, published by Mandatory Reporting Is Not Neutral:[1]

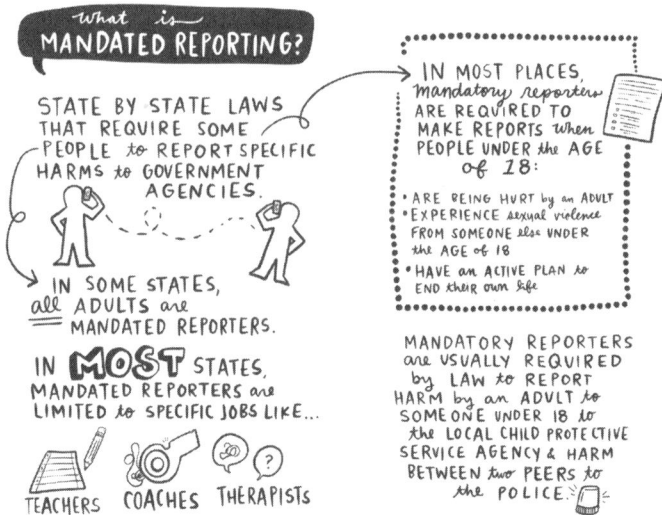

what is MANDATED REPORTING?

STATE BY STATE LAWS THAT REQUIRE SOME PEOPLE to REPORT SPECIFIC HARMS to GOVERNMENT AGENCIES.

IN SOME STATES, all ADULTS are MANDATED REPORTERS.

IN MOST STATES, MANDATORY REPORTERS are LIMITED to SPECIFIC JOBS LIKE...

TEACHERS   COACHES   THERAPISTS

IN MOST PLACES, mandatory reporters ARE REQUIRED TO MAKE REPORTS when PEOPLE UNDER the AGE of 18:

• ARE BEING HURT by an ADULT
• EXPERIENCE sexual violence FROM SOMEONE else UNDER the AGE of 18
• HAVE an ACTIVE PLAN to END their own life

MANDATORY REPORTERS are USUALLY REQUIRED by LAW to REPORT HARM by an ADULT to SOMEONE UNDER 18 to the LOCAL CHILD PROTECTIVE SERVICE AGENCY & HARM BETWEEN two PEERS to the POLICE.

LAWS CAN CHANGE GREATLY FROM PLACE TO PLACE

TO LEARN *more about* *the* LAWS *in your* AREA GO TO:

WWW.MANDATED*reporting* IS NOT NEUTRAL. COM

IN A REPORT CALLED THERE'S NO ONE I CAN TRUST, OVER 3600 PEOPLE SEEKING HELP FOR DOMESTIC VIOLENCE SHARED *their* EXPERIENCES OF MANDATORY REPORTING

THE MAJORITY OF PARTICIPANTS SAID *the* MANDATED REPORT *made the* SITUATION WORSE OR HAD NO IMPACT.

REPORTS LIKE THIS, LIVED *experiences*, & FRONTLINE ADVOCACY HAVE LED ORGANIZERS *to* PROCLAIM THAT...

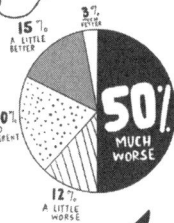

15% A LITTLE BETTER

3% MUCH BETTER

20% NO DIFFERENT

50% MUCH WORSE

12% A LITTLE WORSE

MANDATORY REPORTING *is* NOT NEUTRAL!

IN THIS ZINE, *we* INVITE *you* TO REFLECT & EXPLORE *your* OWN FEELINGS & EXPERIENCES →

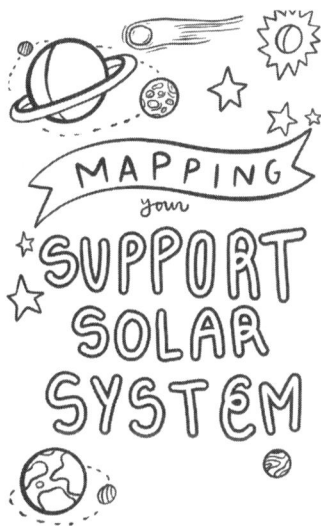

MAPPING *your* SUPPORT SOLAR SYSTEM

instructions

1. MAKE a CIRCLE called "ME" in the middle of the PAGE

2. PLOT A few of your PRIMARY *relationships*:
   • FRIENDS
   • FAMILY (CHOSEN & BIOLOGICAL)
   • TEACHERS
   • NEIGHBORS

3. MAKE LINES of CONNECTION BETWEEN you & your PRIMARY PEOPLE. THE lines MAY look DIFFERENT depending ON the CONNECTION

4. USE + or − symbols TO DESCRIBE the QUALITY of the CONNECTION. OTHER SYMBOLS you CAN USE:

criminalization

surveillance

silencing

policing

IMAGINE MANDATED
REPORTING as a
GIANT SQUID that
ATTACKS COMMUNITIES
(or SHIPS). WHO do you
IMAGINE on the SHIP
& WHAT STRATEGIES
(or TENTACLES) are
IMPACTING them?

COLOR ME!

Coloring page with art by Jamie Harary from *Reimagine Support: A Drug Test Is Not a Parenting Test,* published by Movement for Family Power in 2023.

Illustration by Alexis Neely from *Survival Until Revolution*: *Mandatory Reporting, Anti-Blackness, and Eduction*, published by Mandatory Reporting Is Not Neutral in 2023.

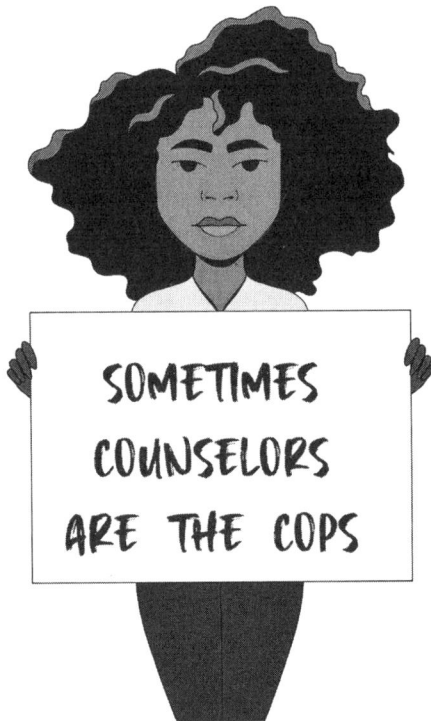

Notes

Introduction: From Outrage to Action

1. "National Data Shows Number of Children in Foster Care Decreases for the Third Consecutive Year," US Department of Health and Human Services, Administration for Children and Families, November 19, 2021, https://www.acf.hhs.gov/media/press/2021/national-data-shows-number-children-foster-care-decreases-third-consecutive-year.

2. Hyunil Kim et al., "Lifetime Prevalence of Investigating Child Maltreatment Among US Children," *American Journal of Public Health* 107, no. 2 (2017), 274–80, https://doi.org/10.2105/AJPH.2016.303545.

3. Anna Arons, "An Unintended Abolition: Family Regulation During the COVID-19 Crisis," *Columbia Journal of Race and Law* 12, no. 1 (2022), http://dx.doi.org/10.2139/ssrn.3815217.

4. Bianca D. M. Wilson et al., *Sexual and Gender Minority Youth in Foster Care*, The Williams Institute, 2014, https://williamsinstitute.law.ucla.edu/publications/sgm-youth-la-foster-care.

5. US Department of Health and Human Services, Administration on Children, Youth, and Families, Children's Bureau, *Child Maltreatment 2023*, 2025, 5, https://www.acf.hhs.gov/cb/data-research/child-maltreatment.

6. See, for example, "Racism at Every Stage: Data Shows How NYC's Administration for Children's Services Discriminates Against Black and Brown Families," New York Civil Liberties Union, June 20, 2023, https://www.nyclu.org/report/

235

racism-every-stage-data-shows-how-nycs-administration-childrens-services-discriminates; Victoria Copeland and Maya Pendleton, *Surveillance of Black Families in the Family Policing System*, upEND Movement, 2022, https://upendmovement.org/wp-content/uploads/2022/06/upEND-Surveillance-06_2022.pdf.

7. US Department of Health and Human Services, *Child Maltreatment 2023*, 9.

8. Andy Newman, "Is N.Y.'s Child Welfare System Racist? Some of Its Own Workers Say Yes," *New York Times*, November 22, 2022, https://www.nytimes.com/2022/11/22/nyregion/nyc-acs-racism-abuse-neglect.html.

9. See, for example, Vivek Sankaran et. al., "A Cure Worse Than the Disease?: The Impact of Removal on Children and Their Families," *Marquette Law Review* 102, no. 4 (2019): 1161, 1194; Allison Eck, "Psychological Damage Inflicted by Parent-Child Separation Is Deep, Long-Lasting," *NOVA Next*, PBS, June 20, 2018, http://www.pbs.org/wgbh/nova/next/body/psychological-damage-inflicted-by-parent-child-separation-is-deep-long-lasting; Sara Goudarzi, "Separating Families May Cause Lifelong Health Damage," *Scientific American,* June 20, 2018, https://www.scientificamerican.com/article/separating-families-may-cause-lifelong-health-damage; William Wan, "What Separation from Parents Does to Children: 'The Effect Is Catastrophic,'" *Washington Post*, June 18, 2018; Ashley Albert et al., "Ending the Family Death Penalty and Building a World We Deserve," *Columbia Journal of Race and Law* 11, no. 3 (2021): 860–94, https://doi.org/10.52214/cjrl.v11i3.8753.

10. See, for example, David Wallace Adams, *Education for Extinction: American Indians and the Boarding School Experience, 1875–1928* (Lawrence: University Press of Kansas), 1995.

11. "Federal Foster Care Financing: How and Why the Current Funding Structure Fails to Meet the Needs of the Child Welfare Field," US Department of Health and Human Services, Office of the Assistant Secretary for Planning and Evaluation, August 2005, https://aspe.

hhs.gov/sites/default/files/migrated_legacy_files//138206/ib.pdf.

12. Emma Peyton Williams and Erica R. Meiners, "Ending the State
    Central Register," *Gender Policy Report*, October 4, 2019, https://
    genderpolicyreport.umn.edu/ending-the-state-central-register/.

13. See, for example, "FAQ: How Do I Find Out If My Name Is on the
    State Child Abuse and Neglect Registry?," Department of Health and
    Human Services, Administration for Children and Families, accessed
    September 6, 2023, https://www.acf.hhs.gov/cb/faq/can10.

14. Tovia Smith, "American Library Association Report
    Says Book Challenges Soared in 2023," NPR, March 14,
    2024, https://www.npr.org/2024/03/14/1238678902/
    book-bans-libraries-american-library-association-schools.

15. Bernice Johnson Reagon, "Coalition Politics: Turning the Century,"
    in *Home Girls: A Black Feminist Anthology*, ed. Barbara Smith (New
    York: Kitchen Table Press, 1983), 343–56.

Chapter 1. It's Never Been About the Welfare of Children: The Origins of the Term *Family Police*

1. Alan J. Dettlaff and Kristen Weber, eds., *Help Is NOT on the Way:
   How Family Policing Perpetuates State Directed Terror*, upEND
   Movement, 2022, https://upendmovement.org/help-is-not-on-the-
   way; Victoria Copeland and Maya Pendleton, "Surveillance of Black
   Families in the Family Policing System," in Detlaff and Weber, *Help Is
   NOT On the Way*, 15–27.

2. Andrew Billingsley and Jeanne M. Giovannoni, *Children of the
   Storm: Black Children and American Child Welfare* (New York:
   Harcourt, Brace, Jovanovich, 1972).

3. Victoria Copeland, "The Complicity of Academia in Policing of
   Families," *The Imprint*, October 20, 2020, https://imprintnews.org/
   opinion/complicity-academia-policing- families/48395; Brianna
   B. Harvey, "Carceral Entanglements: Exploring the Educational
   Experiences of Black Youth in Foster Care," presentation at the
   Annual Conference of Ford Foundation Fellows, Virtual Conference,

October 9, 2020.

4. For movements against the PIC, see, for example, Ruth Wilson Gilmore, "In the Shadow of the Shadow State," in *The Revolution Will Not Be Funded*, eds. INCITE! (Durham, NC: Duke University Press, 2017), 41–52; Mariame Kaba, *We Do This 'Til We Free Us: Abolitionist Organizing and Transforming Justice* (Chicago: Haymarket Books, 2021); Angela Y. Davis, *Are Prisons Obsolete?* (New York: Seven Stories, 2003); Victoria A. Copeland and Alan J. Dettlaff, "Family Policing and the Carceral State: How Carceral Violence Persists Through the Surveillance, Punishment, and Regulation of Families," *Journal of Progressive Human Services* (December 4, 2024): 1–20.

5. Tarek Z. Ismail, "Family Policing and the Fourth Amendment," *California Law Review* 111 (2023).

6. "Addressing Disproportionality, Disparity, and Equity Throughout Child Welfare," Child Welfare Information Gateway, Department of Health and Human Services, Administration for Children and Families, n.d., https://www.acf.hhs.gov/cb/focus-areas/equity.

7. "Mandated Reporting," Child Welfare Information Gateway, Department of Health and Human Services, Administration for Children and Families, n.d., https://www.childwelfare.gov/topics/safety-and-risk/mandated-reporting.

8. Brianna Harvey et al., "'Ain't Nobody About to Trap Me': The Violence of Multi-System Collusion and Entrapment for Incarcerated Disabled Girls of Color," *Journal of School Violence* 23, no. 2 (2024): 202–19.

9. Angelique Brown, "Orphan Trains (1854–1929)," Social Welfare History Project, https://socialwelfare.library.vcu.edu/programs/child-welfarechild-labor/orphan-trains.

10. "Indian Boarding Schools," National Indian Child Welfare Association, May 19, 2022, https://www.nicwa.org/boarding-schools.

11. On Black family separations, see, for example, "Black Families

Severed by Slavery," Equal Justice Initiative, January 29, 2018, https://eji.org/news/history-racial-injustice-black-families-severed-by-slavery; Josie Pickens, "No Coincidence: Black Family Separations Then and Now," upEND, February 16, 2023, https://upendmovement.org/2023/02/16/no-coincidence.

12. Erin Blakemore, "Jim Crow Laws Created 'Slavery by Another Name,'" *National Geographic*, February 5, 2020, https://www.nationalgeographic.com/history/article/jim-crow-laws-created-slavery-another-name.

13. Julilly Kohler-Hausmann, *Getting Tough: Welfare and Imprisonment in 1970s America* (Princeton, NJ: Princeton University Press, 2019).

14. Ellen Reese, *Backlash Against Welfare Mothers: Past and Present* (Berkeley: University of California Press, 2005).

15. Jasmine Wali, "Where Were the Social Workers? A Historical Overview of the Social Work Profession's Complicity in the Family Policing System," *Columbia Social Work Review* 21, no. 1 (2023): 121–40, https://doi.org/10.52214/cswr.v21i1.11210.

16. Angela Burton and Angeline Montauban, "Toward Community Control of Child Welfare Funding: Repeal the Child Abuse Prevention and Treatment Act and Delink Child Protection from Family Well-Being," *Columbia Journal of Race and Law* 11, no. 3 (2021).

17. Felicia Kornbluh, *The Battle for Welfare Rights: Politics and Poverty in Modern America* (Philadelphia: University of Pennsylvania Press, 2007).

18. Kristina Rosinsky et al., *Child Welfare Financing SFY 2020, a Survey of Federal, State, and Local Expenditures*, Child Trends, May 2023, https://cms.childtrends.org/wp-content/uploads/2023/04/ChildWelfareFinancingReport_ChildTrends_May2023.pdf.

19. Anna Arons, "An Unintended Abolition: Family Regulation During the COVID-19 Crisis," *Columbia Journal of Race and Law* 12, no. 1 (2022).

20. Shanta Trivedi, "The Harm of Child Removal," *New York University Review of Law and Social Change* 43 (2019), 523–80.

21. "Cops, Group Homes and Criminalized Kids," *The Imprint*, January 21, 2015, https://imprintnews.org/news-2/cops-group-homes-and-criminalized-kids/9109.

22. Rachael J. Keefe et al., "Psychotropic Medication Prescribing: Youth in Foster Care Compared with Other Medicaid Enrollees," *Journal of Child and Adolescent Psychopharmacology* 33, no. 4 (2023): 149–55, https://doi.org/10.1089/cap.2022.0092.

23. Peggy Cooper Davis, *Neglected Stories: The Constitution and Family Values* (New York: Hill and Wang, 1998).

24. Amelia M. Biehl and Brian Hill, "Foster Care and the Earned Income Tax Credit," *Review of Economics of the Household* 16, no. 3 (2018): 661–80, https://doi.org/10.1007/s11150-017-9381-1; Nicole L. Kovski et al., "Short-Term Effects of Tax Credits on Rates of Child Maltreatment Reports in the United States," *Pediatrics* 150, no. 1 (2022), https://doi.org/10.1542/peds.2021-054939; Kerri M. Raissian and Lindsey R. Bullinger, "Money Matters: Does the Minimum Wage Affect Child Maltreatment Rates?," *Children and Youth Services Review* 72 (2017), 60–70, https://doi.org/10.1016/j.childyouth.2016.09.033; Emily C. B. Brown et al., "Assessment of Rates of Child Maltreatment in States with Medicaid Expansion vs. States Without Medicaid Expansion," *JAMA Network Open* 2, no. 6 (2019), https://doi.org/10.1001/jamanetworkopen.2019.5529; Mi-Youn Yang et al., "Child Care Subsidy and Child Maltreatment," *Child and Family Social Work* 24, no. 4 (2019), 547–54, https://doi.org/10.1111/cfs.12635.

Chapter 2. Who Is Safe? Who Is Protected?

1. Maya Angelou, "Million Man March Poem" (1995), available at Allpoetry.com, https://allpoetry.com/Million-Man-March-Poem.

2. Kwame Ture and Charles V. Hamilton, *Black Power: The Politics of Liberation* (New York: Vintage, 1967).

3. *Kerner Commission Report on the Causes, Events, and Aftermaths of Civil Disorders of 1967*, https://belonging.berkeley.edu/sites/default/

files/kerner_commission_full_report.pdf.

4. For more on the Kerner Commission, see Jelani Cobb, ed., *The Essential Kerner Commission Report* (New York: Liveright, 2021).

5. For more on punitive welfare policies and practices see Kaaryn Gustafson, *Cheating Welfare: Public Assistance and the Criminalization of Poverty* (New York: New York University Press, 2011).

Chapter 3. Prevention, Reparations, and Reunification: Black Families and Healing the Harms of Family Policing

1. Dorothy Roberts, "Building a World Without Family Policing," LPE Project, July 17, 2023, https://lpeproject.org/blog/building-a-world-without-family-policing; Dorothy Roberts, *Torn Apart: How the Child Welfare System Destroys Black Families—and How Abolition Can Build a Safer World* (New York: Basic Books, 2022); "US Indian Boarding School History," National Native American Boarding School Healing Coalition, 2019, https://boardingschoolhealing. org/education/us-indian-boarding-school-history; Alan J. Dettlaff, *Confronting the Racist Legacy of the American Child Welfare System: The Case for Abolition* (New York: Oxford University Press, 2023); Alan J. Dettlaff et al., "Emerging Issues at the Intersection of Immigration and Child Welfare," *Child Welfare* 88, no. 2 (2009): 47–67; "Hearing Wrap Up: ORR Director Fails to Answer Questions About 85,000 Lost Unaccompanied Alien Children, Flawed Vetting of Sponsors, and More," US House of Representatives Oversight Committee, April 18, 2023, https://oversight.house.gov/ release/hearing-wrap-up-orr-director-fails-to-answer-questions-about-85000-lost-unaccompanied-alien-children-flawed-vetting-of-sponsors-and-more%EF%BF%BC.

2. Alan J. Dettlaff and Reiko Boyd, "Racial Disproportionality and Disparities in the Child Welfare System: Why Do They Exist, and What Can Be Done to Address Them?," *Annals of the American Academy of Political and Social Science* 692, no. 1 (2020): 253–74.

3. Dorothy Roberts, "Caseworker Files—Race and Class in the Child Welfare System," PBS, n.d., https://www.pbs.org/wgbh/pages/frontline/shows/fostercare/caseworker/roberts.html.

4. Jazmyn Luckett, "The 'Black Welfare Queen' and the Incarceration of Black Mothers in Modern America," Gender and Sexuality in World History, 2022, https://genderhistory.pubpub.org/pub/welfare-queen-incarceration-black-mothers; Margaret M. C. Thomas, Jane Waldfogel, and Ovita F. Williams, "Inequities in Child Protective Services Contact Between Black and White Children," *Child Maltreatment* 28, no. 1 (2023): 42–54.

5. Sydney L. Goetz, "From Removal to Incarceration: How the Modern Child Welfare System and Its Unintended Consequences Catalyzed the Foster Care-to-Prison Pipeline," *University of Maryland Law Journal of Race, Religion, Gender, and Class* 20 (2020): 289; Patrick J. Fowler et al.,"Pathways to and from Homelessness and Associated Psychosocial Outcomes Among Adolescents Leaving the Foster Care System," *American Journal of Public Health* 99, no. 8 (2009): 1453–58; "The Prison Industrial Complex: Mapping Private Sector Players," Worth Rises, 2019, https://worthrises.org/theprisonindustry2019; *The Business of Homelessness: Financial and Human Costs of the Shelter-Industrial Complex*, Picture the Homeless Research Committee, 2018, https://nyf.issuelab.org/resource/the-business-of-homelessness-financial-and-human-costs-of-the-shelter-industrial-complex.html.

6. Dorothy Roberts, *Shattered Bonds: The Color of Child Welfare* (New York: Basic Books, 2002).

7. Thomas M. C. Thomas, Jane Waldfogel, and Ovita F. Williams, "Inequities in Child Protective Services Contact Between Black and White Children," *Child Maltreatment* 28, no. 1 (February 2023): 42–54.

8. "Reformist Reforms vs. Abolitionist Steps in Policing," Critical Resistance, 2020, https://criticalresistance.org/resources/reformist-reforms-vs-abolitionist-steps-in-policing.

9. Maya Pendleton et al., "Framework for Evaluating Reformist Reforms vs. Abolitionist Steps to End the Family Policing System," upEND Movement, 2023, https://upendmovement.org/wp-content/uploads/2023/01/upEND-abolitionist-framework-01-2023.pdf; "Mandated Supporting," JMACforFamilies, 2023, https://jmacforfamilies.org/mandated-supporting; "End Surveillance of Families," upEND Movement, 2023, https://upendmovement.org/end-surveillance-families.

10. State central / child protective registries are arbitrary registries organized by the state that label family members as "indicated for neglect," often with low standards of evidence for placement on registries, and decades to lifetime restrictions for people on the registries to provide care for or gain custody of children in their families, adopt a child, or work in childcare. Recent advocacy has moved to pass bills at the state level that would require a "preponderance of evidence" beyond "some credible evidence" for a person to be placed on a registry; "New Law Reforming NY State Central Registry Will Provide Justice and Relief to Families," JMACforFamilies, 2020, https://jmacforfamilies.org/news3.

11. Roberts, *Shattered Bonds*.

12. Wendy A. Bach, *Prosecuting Poverty, Criminalizing Care* (Cambridge, UK: Cambridge University Press, 2022).

13. "Policing by Another Name: Mandated Reporting as State Surveillance," Shriver Center on Poverty Law, 2020, https://www.povertylaw.org/wp-content/uploads/2020/11/spotlight-foster-system-webinar-2-policing.pdf; Dorothy Roberts, "Abolishing Policing Also Means Abolishing Family Regulation," *The Imprint*, June 16, 2020, https://imprintnews.org/child-welfare-2/abolishing-policing-also-means-abolishing-family-regulation/44480; Shira Hassan, *Saving Our Own Lives: A Liberatory Practice of Harm Reduction* (Chicago: Haymarket Books, 2022).

14. Christopher Wimer et al., "Food Assistance Can Disrupt

Intergenerational Poverty in the United States, Promoting Racial Economic Equity," *Equitable Growth*, May 30, 2023, https://equitablegrowth.org/food-assistance-can-disrupt-intergenerational-poverty-in-the-united-states-promoting-racial-economic-equity; "Transform Societal Conditions So Families and Communities Can Thrive," upEND Movement, 2023, https://upendmovement.org/transform-societal-conditions-families-communities-can-thrive.

15. Movement for Family Power, NYU Family Defense Clinic, and Drug Policy Alliance, "How the Foster System Has Become Ground Zero for the U.S. Drug War," Movement for Family Power, 2020, https://www.movementforfamilypower.org/ground-zero.

16. Elisa Minoff, "Entangled Roots: The Role of Race in Policies That Separate Families," *Center for the Study of Social Policy*, November 2018, https://cssp.org/resource/entangled-roots.

17. Rachel Treisman, "Evanston, Ill., Approves Historic Reparations Plan for Black Residents," NPR, March 23, 2021, https://www.npr.org/2021/03/23/980277688/in-likely-first-chicago-suburb-of-evanston-approves-reparations-for-black-reside; Tasseli McKay, *Stolen Wealth, Hidden Power: The Case for Reparations for Mass Incarceration* (Oakland: University of California Press, 2022); Amelia F. Meyer and Jessica Pryce, "Child Welfare Needs a Truth, Reconciliation, and Reparation Process," *The Imprint*, March 8, 2021, https://imprintnews.org/child-welfare-2/truth-reconciliation-reparation-child-welfare/52475.

18. "Reparations Now Toolkit," Movement for Black Lives, 2019, https://m4bl.org/wp-content/uploads/2020/05/Reparations-Now-Toolkit-FINAL.pdf.

19. Shira Hassan, *Saving Our Own Lives: A Liberatory Practice of Harm Reduction* (Chicago: Haymarket Books, 2022).

20. "Resolution Adopted by the General Assembly on 16 December 2005. 60/147. Basic Principles and Guidelines on the Right to a Remedy and Reparation for Victims of

Gross Violations of International Human Rights Law and
Serious Violations of International Humanitarian Law,"
United Nations General Assembly, 2006, https://www.
ohchr.org/en/instruments-mechanisms/instruments/
basic-principles-and-guidelines-right-remedy-and-reparation.

Chapter 4. Young People Deserve Community Care

1. When I was a child, this government agency responsible for family
    policing in the State of New Jersey was called Division of Youth and
    Family Services (DYFS); it is now called Division of Child Protection
    and Permanency (DCPP).

2. US Department of Health and Human Services, *Street Outreach
    Program: Data Collection Project Executive Summary*, October
    2014.

3. "LGBTQ Youth Homelessness," National Network for Youth, 2023,
    https://nn4youth.org/lgbtq-homeless-youth; "LGBTQ Youth in the
    Foster Care System," Human Rights Campaign, 2015, https://hrc-
    prod-requests.s3-us-west2.amazonaws.com/files/assets/resources/
    HRC-YouthFosterCare-IssueBrief-FINAL.pdf.

4. Talila A. Lewis, "Working Definition of Ableism—January 2022
    Update," January 1, 2022, https://www.talilalewis.com/blog/
    working-definition-of-ableism-january-2022-update.

5. Bernadine Waller et al.,"Racial Inequities in Homicide Rates and
    Homicide Methods Among Black and White Women Aged 25–44
    Years in the USA, 1999–2020: A Cross-Sectional Time Series
    Study," *The Lancet* 403, no. 10,430 (March 9, 2024), https://doi.
    org/10.1016/S0140-6736(23)02279-1.

6. Generation FIVE, *Ending Childhood Sexism: A Transformative Justice
    Guidebook*, 2017.

7. Parenting Decolonized (@prntgdcolonized), X, 2022, https://x.
    com/prntgdcolonized/status/1561353934706511873.

8. "Principles of Unity," INCITE! Women of Color Against Violence,

n.d., https://incite-national.org/principles-of-unity.

9. C. Parks, "He Came Out as Trans. Then Texas Had Him Investigate Parents of Trans Kids," *Washington Post*, September 23, 2022, https://www.washingtonpost.com/dc-md-va/2022/09/23/texas-transgender-child-abuse-investigations.

10. Audre Lorde, "A Litany for Survival," *The Black Unicorn: Poems* (New York: W. W. Norton, 1978).

11. Mia Mingus, "Pods: The Building Blocks of Transformative Justice and Collective Care," SOIL: A Transformative Justice Project, March 16, 2023. https://www.soiltjp.org/our-work/resources/pods.

12. Queenie's Crew, *Building Communities of Care: An Activity Book*, available at queeniescrew.com.

Chapter 6. Who Do You Tell?

1. "Preventing Sexual Violence," Centers for Disease Control and Prevention, June 22, 2022, https://www.cdc.gov/violenceprevention/sexualviolence/fastfact.html.

2. C. A. Rennison, "Rape and Sexual Assault: Reporting to Police and Medical Attention, 1992–2000 [NCJ 194530]," 2022, retrieved from the US Department of Justice, Office of Justice Programs, Bureau of Justice Statistics, http://bjs.ojp.usdoj.gov/content/pub/pdf/rsarp00.pdf.

3. Leigh Goodmark, "Gender-Based Violence, Law Reform, and the Criminalization of Survivors of Violence," *International Journal for Crime, Justice, and Social Democracy* 10, no. 4 (2021): 13–25.

4. Caroline Harlow, "Prior Abuse Reported by Inmates and Probationers," US Department of Justice, April 1999, https://bjs.ojp.gov/content/pub/pdf/parip.pdf.

5. For more about the history and context of CAPTA, see "About CAPTA: A Legislative History," Child Welfare Information Gateway, US Department of Health and Human Services, Administration for Children and Families, 2019; Leonard G. Brown III and Kevin

Gallagher, "Mandatory Reporting of Abuse: A Historical Perspective
on the Evolution of States' Current Mandatory Reporting Laws with
a Review of the Laws in the Commonwealth of Pennsylvania, 59 Vill.
L. Rev. Tolle Lege 37," 2014, available at https://digitalcommons.law.
villanova.edu/vlr/vol59/iss6/5.
6. "Child Maltreatment 2022," US Department of Health and Human
Services, Administration for Children and Families, 2024, https://
www.acf.hhs.gov/cb/data-research/child-maltreatment.
7. "Child Maltreatment 2022."
8. "National Crime Victimization Survey, 2010–2016," Department of
Justice, Office of Justice Programs, Bureau of Justice Statistics, 2017.

Chapter 7. The Community Dimensions of State Child Protection

1. Dorothy Roberts, *Shattered Bonds: The Color of Child Welfare* (New
York: Basic Books, 2002).
2. Roberts, *Shattered Bonds*, 8; Alfred Pérez et al., "Demographics of
Children in Foster Care," Pew Charitable Trusts, 2003; Center for
the Study of Social Policy, The Race and Child Welfare Project, "Fact
Sheet 1: Basic Facts on Disproportionate Representation of African
Americans in the Foster Care System," 2004.
3. "The AFCARS Report, Preliminary FY 2022 Estimates as of May
9, 2023—No. 30," US Department of Health and Human Services,
May 9, 2023, 2; "America's Children: Key National Indicators of
Well-Being, 2023," Federal Interagency Forum on Child and Family
Statistics, 2023, xi.
4. Christopher Wildeman and Natalia Emanuel, "Cumulative Risks
of Foster Care Placement by Age 18 for US Children, 2000–2011,"
PLOS One 9, no. 3 (2014): e92785.
5. Jason Baron et al., "Racial Discrimination in Child Protection
(NBER Working Paper 3149)," National Bureau of Economic
Research, October 1, 2023.

6. "Youth in Care by Demographic," Illinois Department of Children and Family Services, April 30, 2024, https://dcfs.illinois.gov/content/dam/soi/en/web/dcfs/documents/about-us/reports-and-statistics/documents/youth-in-care-by-demographic.pdf.

7. "Report on Youth in Foster Care, 2023," US Department of Health and Human Services, Administration for Children's Services, December 31, 2023.

8. "Foster Care: Temporary Out-of-Home Care for Children," Minnesota Department of Human Services, n.d., https://edocs.dhs.state.mn.us/lfserver/Public/DHS-4760-ENG.

9. Robert B. Hill, "Overrepresentation of Children of Color in Foster Care in 2000," Working Paper no. 6, Race Matters Consortium, November 2004.

10. Hill, "Overrepresentation of Children of Color in Foster Care."

11. David B. Mitchell, "Building a Multidisciplinary, Collaborative Child Protection System: The Challenge to Law Schools," *Family Court Review* 41, no. 4 (2003): 432, 436.

12. Robert J. Sampson, "Transcending Tradition: New Directions in Community Research, Chicago Style," *Criminology* 40, no. 2 (2002): 213, 219–20, 222; Robert J. Sampson et al., "Assessing 'Neighborhood Effects': Social Processes and New Directions in Research," *Annual Review of Sociology* 28 (2002): 443, 446, 457–58, 465.

13. William Julius Wilson, *The Truly Disadvantaged: The Inner City, the Underclass, and Public Policy* (Chicago: University of Chicago Press, 1987), 12, 135–36.

14. Wilson, *Truly Disadvantaged*, 58.

15. Todd. R. Clear et al., "Coercive Mobility and Crime: A Preliminary Examination of Concentrated Incarceration and Social Disorganization," *Justice Quarterly* 20, no. 1 (2003): 33, 46, 57; Robert J. Sampson et al., "Neighborhoods and Violent Crime: A Multilevel Study of Collective Efficacy," *Science* 277 (1997): 918, 921–23.

16. Robert J. Sampson, "How Do Communities Undergird or Undermine Human Development? Relevant Contexts and Social Mechanisms," in *Does It Take a Village?: Community Effects on Children, Adolescents, and Families*, eds. Alan Booth and Ann C. Crouter (Philadelphia: Taylor & Francis, 2001), 3, 6; Jeanne Brooks-Gunn et al., "Do Neighborhoods Influence Child and Adolescent Development?," *American Journal of Sociology* 99, no.2 (1992): 353.

17. Sampson et al., "Neighborhoods and Violent Crime," 918, 923.

18. "Transforming Neighborhoods into Family-Supporting Environments: Evaluation Issues and Challenges," Annie E. Casey Foundation, September 25, 2000.

19. OMG Center for Collaborative Learning, "A Community Takes on Child Welfare Service Delivery: A Case Study of Community-Based System Reform in Ward Seven of the District of Columbia," 2, 2002.

20. OMG Center, "A Community Takes on Child Welfare Service Delivery," 28; Cheryl A. Hosley, Linda Gensheimer, and Mai Yang, "Building Effective Working Relationships Across Culturally and Ethnically Diverse Communities," *Child Welfare* 82, no. 2 (2003): 157.

21. Brian Wharf, "Building a Case for Community Approaches to Child Welfare," in *Community Work Approaches to Child Welfare*, ed. Brian Wharf (Toronto: University of Toronto Press, 2002), 181, 191–92.

22. James P. Connell and Anne C. Kubisch, "Community Approaches to Improving Outcomes for Urban Children, Youth, and Families: Current Trends and Future Directions," in Booth and Crouter, *Does It Take a Village?*, 177.

23. Marie O. Weil, "Community Building: Building Community Practice," *Social Work* 41, no. 5 (1996): 481, 485.

24. Robert J. Chaskin, "The Evaluation of 'Community Building': Measuring the Social Effects of Community-Based Practice," in *Assessing Outcomes in Child and Family Services: Comparative Design and Policy Issues*, eds. Anthony N. Maluccio et al. (New York: Routledge, 2002), 28.

25. Casey Foundation, "Transforming Neighborhoods," 38–44.

26. Caterina Gouvis Roman and Gretchen E. Moore, "Measuring Local Institutions and Organizations: The Role of Community Institutional Capacity in Social Capacity," *Urban Institute*, May 3, 2004.

27. Sampson, "How Do Communities Undergird or Undermine Human Development?," 10; Barrett A. Lee, "Taking Neighborhoods Seriously," in Booth and Crouter, *Does It Take a Village?*, 31, 35.

28. Robert M. George and Bong J. Lee, "The Entry of Children from the Welfare System into Foster Care: Differences by Race," in *Race Matters in Child Welfare: The Overrepresentation Of African American Children In The System*, eds. Dennette M. Derezotes et al. (Washington, DC: Child Welfare League of America, 2004); Mark E. Courtney et al., "Race and Child Welfare Services: Past Research and Future Directions," *Child Welfare* 75, no. 2 (1996): 99; Wendy G. Lane et al., "Racial Differences in the Evaluation of Pediatric Fractures for Physical Abuse," *Journal of the American Medical Association* 288, no. 13 (2002): 1603; "Report to the Legislature," Minnesota Department of Human Services, Children's Services Administration.

29. Alyssa Katz, "Mommy Nearest," *City Limits*, June 2000, https://citylimits.org/2000/06/01/mommy-nearest.

30. Roberts, *Shattered Bonds*, 240; "Youth in Care by Zip Code," Illinois Department of Child and Family Services, April 30, 2024, https://dcfs.illinois.gov/content/dam/soi/en/web/dcfs/documents/about-us/reports-and-statistics/documents/youth-in-care-by-zip-code.pdf.

31. Courtney et al., "Race and Child Welfare Services," 100; Andrea Charlow, "Race, Poverty, and Neglect," *William Mitchell Law Review* 28, no. 2 (2001): 763, 765.

32. Dorothy Roberts, "The Racial Geography of Child Welfare: Toward a New Research Paradigm," *Child Welfare* 87, no. 2 (2008): 125–50; Kelley Fong, "Neighborhood Inequality in the Prevalence of

Reported and Substantiated Child Maltreatment," *Child Abuse and Neglect* 90 (2019): 13–21.

33. Linda Gordon, *Pitied but Not Entitled: Single Mothers and the History of Welfare* (Cambridge, MA: Harvard University Press, 1998), 39–40.

34. Gordon, *Pitied but Not Entitled*, 43.

35. Gordon, *Pitied but Not Entitled*, 40.

36. Gordon, *Pitied but Not Entitled*, 39, 45–48.

37. Dorothy Roberts, "Black Club Women and Child Welfare: Lessons for Modern Reform," *Florida State University Law Review* 32, no. 3 (2005).

38. Martin Guggenheim, "Somebody's Children: Sustaining the Family's Place in Child Welfare Policy," *Harvard Law Review* 113, no. 7 (2000): 1746.

39. Jane Waldfogel, *The Future of Child Protection: How to Break the Cycle of Abuse and Neglect* (Cambridge, MA: Harvard University Press, 1998), 139.

40. Waldfogel, *Future of Child Protection*, 139.

41. Adoption and Safe Families Act of 1997, Pub. L. No. 105-89, §§ 101, 111 (1997).

42. Kurtis A. Kemper, annotation, *Construction and Application by State Courts of the Federal Adoption and Safe Families Act and Its Implementing Statutes*, 2003 American Law Reports 5th, 3, 4 (2005) (collecting and analyzing state cases in which the ASFA and implementing state statutes have been construed or applied).

43. Richard A. Posner, "An Economic Theory of the Criminal Law," *Columbia Law Review* 85, no. 6 (1985): 1193.

44. Kemper, *Construction and Application by State Courts*, 3, 4.

45. Courtney et al., "Race and Child Welfare Services," 99; Matthew Mason et. al., "A Comparison of Foster Care Outcomes Across Four Child Welfare Agencies," *Journal of Family Social Work* 7, no. 2 (2003): 55.

46. Douglas Massey, "The Prodigal Paradigm Returns: Ecology Comes Back to Sociology," in Booth and Crouter, *Does It Take a Village?*, 41–42.

47. Andrew Billingsley and Cleopatra Howard Caldwell, "The Church, the Family, and the School in the African American Community," *Journal of Negro Education* 60, no. 3 (1991): 427; Marc Mauer, "Thinking About Prison and Its Impact in the Twenty-First Century," *Ohio State Journal of Criminal Law* 2 (2005): 607.

48. Harriet Ward, "Current Initiatives in the Development of Outcome-Based Evaluation of Children's Services," in *Assessing Outcomes in Child and Family Services: Comparative Design and Policy Issues*, eds. Anthony N. Maluccio et al. (New York: Routledge, 2002), 6; Lois Wright and Kathy Paget, "A Learning-Organization Approach to Evaluation," in Ward, *Assessing Outcomes*, 127.

49. Wright and Paget, "A Learning-Organization Approach," 127.

50. Julia P. Fortier and Dawn Bishop, "Setting the Agenda for Research on Cultural Competence in Health Care," US Department of Health and Human Services, August 2004, 9.

51. Margaret S. Sherraden and Uma A. Segal, "Multicultural Issues in Child Welfare," *Children and Youth Services Review* 18, no. 6 (1996): 497, 502.

52. Roberts, *Shattered Bonds*, 236–54.

53. Dorothy Roberts, *Torn Apart: How the Child Welfare System Destroys Black Families—and How Abolition Can Build a Safer World* (New York: Basic Books, 2022); Kelley Fong, *Investigating Families: Motherhood in the Shadow of Child Protective Services* (Princeton, NJ: Princeton University Press, 2023).

54. Alan J. Dettlaff and Kristen Weber, eds., *Help Is NOT on the Way: How Family Policing Perpetuates State Directed Terror*, upEND Movement, 2022, https://upendmovement.org/help-is-not-on-the-way; "Our Mission and Approach," Movement for Family Power, https://www.movementforfamilypower.org/our-mission-and-approach.

55. Dorothy Roberts, "The Social and Moral Cost of Mass Incarceration in African American Communities," *Stanford Law*

Review 56, no. 5 (2004): 1271.

56. Clear et al., "Coercive Mobility and Crime," 33, 46, 57; Jeffrey Fagan, Valerie West, and Jan Holland, "Reciprocal Effects of Crime and Incarceration in New York City Neighborhoods," *Fordham Urban Law Journal* 30, no. 5 (2003): 1551–54, 1568–69.
57. Fagan et al., "Reciprocal Effects of Crime," 1553–56.
58. Roberts, "The Racial Geography of Child Welfare."
59. Roberts, *Shattered Bonds*, 240.

Chapter 8. Beyond Mandated Reporting: Organizing from the Inside Out

1. Throughout this chapter we use the term *social worker* to include mental health providers of all types.
2. We are deeply grateful to Arash, Ayla, Emma, Jasmine, Keya, Maria, Talia, and Veronica, leaders and thought partners in the MRAMR space, as well as each and every person in the MRAMR community. The following chapter would not be possible without all of you.
3. While mandated reporting harms communities of color disproportionately more than white families, the current and historic impact is even more disproportionately felt in Black and Indigenous communities.
4. Following how directly impacted people describe their lived experience, we use the term *family policing* in place of what has traditionally been referred to as the child welfare/protection system.
5. Alan J. Dettlaff and Laura Abrams, "An Open Letter to NASW and Allied Organizations on Social Work's Relationship with Law Enforcement," *Medium*, January 20, 2021.
6. "Child Welfare Data Monitoring and Analysis Profiles (MAPS)," Office of Children and Family Services, New York State, 2022, https://ocfs.ny.gov/main/reports/maps.
7. Carrie Lippy et al., "There's No One I Can Trust: The Impact of Mandatory Reporting on the Help-Seeking and Well-Being of

Domestic Violence Survivors," National LGBTQ DV Capacity Building Learning Center, 2016, https://vawnet.org/sites/default/files/assets/files/LGBTQDVCapacityBuildingLearningCenter-TheresNoOneICanTrust-2016.pdf.

8. "Narrowing the Front Door to NYC's Child Welfare System Report and Community Recommendations," Narrowing the Front Door, December 2022, https://www.narrowingthefrontdoor.org/_files/ugd/9c5953_2a2cf809f5d34d989b7ec4459e72930a.pdf.

9. "Narrowing the Front Door."

10. Andy Newman, "Is N.Y.'s Child Welfare System Racist? Some of Its Own Workers Say Yes," *New York Times*, November 22, 2022, https://www.nytimes.com/2022/11/22/nyregion/nyc-acs-racism-abuse-neglect.html.

11. Angela Butel, review of *Data Brief: Child Welfare Investigations*, Center for New York City Affairs, The New School, accessed March 22, 2024, http://www.centernyc.org/data-brief-child-welfare-investigations.

12. Dorothy Roberts, *Torn Apart: How the Child Welfare System Destroys Black Families—and How Abolition Can Build a Safer World* (New York: Basic Books, 2022).

13. "Structure—Radical Social Work Group," Radical Social Work Group, accessed April 30, 2024, https://radicalsocialworkgroup.tumblr.com; Frederic Reamer, "Moral Injury in Social Work," *Families in Society: The Journal of Contemporary Social Services* 103, no. 3.

14. "Code of Ethics," National Association of Social Workers, 2021, https://www.socialworkers.org/About/Ethics/Code-of-Ethics/Code-of-Ethics-English.

15. Reamer, "Moral Injury in Social Work."

16. Victoria Williamson et al., "Moral Injury: The Effect on Mental Health and Implications for Treatment," *The Lancet Psychiatry* 8, no. 6 (2021), https://doi.org/10.1016/s2215-0366(21)00113-9.

17. For free access to the *Alternatives to Mandated Reporting Guide*, email beyondmandatedreporting@gmail.com.

18. Mia Mingus, "Pods and Pod Mapping Worksheet," Bay Area

Transformative Justice Collective, June 2, 2016, https://batjc.
wordpress.com/resources/pods-and-pod-mapping-worksheet.

19. See, for example, Jasmine Wali, "'I'd Rather Take a Beating Than Catch
a CPS Case': Survivors Face an Impossible Choice," *The Nation*, April
5, 2023, https://www.thenation.com/article/society/child-welfare-
domestic-violence; Talia Gruber, "Beyond Mandated Reporting:
Debunking Assumptions to Support Children and Families,"
Abolitionist Perspectives in Social Work 1, no. 1 (2023), https://apsw-
ojs-uh.tdl.org/apsw/article/view/12.

Chapter 9. "I'm Not an Organizer, I Just Organized"

1. In 1963, construction of Downstate Medical Center in East Flatbush
was supposed to provide an economic labor boost to the borough.
However, the construction contracts were given to unions that
did not permit Black membership. Congress of Racial Equality
(CORE) and a dozen of Brooklyn's most prominent Black ministers
organized protests to demand an end to racial discrimination in the
unions. "Bodies on the Line," Brooklyn Library, n.d., https://www.
bklynlibrary.org/brooklyn-resists/exhibition/bodies-on-the-line.

2. In 1968, Black and Puerto Rican parents organized for better schools.
This resulted in community-controlled schools in New York. "May
9, 1968: Ocean Hill-Brownsville Teachers' Strike of 1968," Zinn
Education Project, n.d., https://www.zinnedproject.org/news/tdih/
ocean-hill-brownsville/.

3. The International Wages for Housework Campaign (IWFHC)
is a grassroots women's network campaigning for recognition
and payment for all caring work. Between 1974 and 1976, three
autonomous organizations formed within the Wages for Housework
Campaign in the UK, US, and Canada: Wages Due Lesbians (now
Queer Strike), the English Collective of Prostitutes, and Black
Women for Wages for Housework. "The Campaign for Wages for
Housework," Global Women's Strike, accessed May 28, 2024, https://
globalwomenstrike.net/wagesforhousework.

4. "Give Us Back Our Children," Global Women's Strike, n.d., https://globalwomenstrike.net/give-us-back-our-children.

5. "DCFS: Give Us Back Our Children! (2012)," YouTube, September 17, 2012, https://www.youtube.com/watch?v=1WE70juWEYY.

6. Operation Stop CPS, n.d., https://www.operationstopcps.com.

7. The City University of New York (CUNY) implemented an open admissions policy in 1970 allowing anyone with a high school diploma or equivalent to be admitted regardless of their academic background or qualifications. "1961–1969: The Creation of CUNY—Open Admissions Struggle," CUNY Digital History Archive, n.d., https://cdha.cuny.edu/coverage/coverage/show/id/23.

8. Selma James was the cofounder of the International Wages for Housework Campaign and coordinator of the Global Women's Strike. Mariarosa Dalla Costa and Selma James, *The Power of Women and the Subversion of the Community* (Bristol, UK: Falling Wall Press, 1975). Wages for housework was one of the six demands in Selma James, "Women, the Unions and Work, or What Is Not to Be Done," *Radical America* 7, nos. 4–5 (1973): 51–71.

9. Lyndsey Jenkins, "'There Has Always Been a Black Women's Peace Movement': Women of Colour and Anti-War Activism in the U.S., 1968–1972—Frankie Chappell," Women's History Network, October 4, 2021, https://womenshistorynetwork.org/there-has-always-been-a-black-womens-peace-movement-by-frankie-chappell; "Black Women for Wages for Housework," Global Women's Strike, n.d., https://globalwomenstrike.net/blackwomenforwagesforhousework.

10. "No Cuts, Just Bucks—Black Women for Wages for Housework," Rise Up! A Digital Archive of Feminist Activism, Global Women's Strike, n.d., https://riseupfeministarchive.ca/culture/buttons/button-mp-blackwomen-wagesforhousework.

11. Beulah Sanders was a welfare rights activist and organizer in the 1960s and 1970s. She was chair of the New York Citywide Coordinating Committee of Welfare Groups and became a founding member and vice president of the National Welfare Rights Organization.

"Education: Beulah Sanders Way: Organizing for Welfare Rights," YouTube, March 18, 2019, https://www.youtube.com/watch?v=cvMQz7CcBnM.

Johnnie Tillmon was an American welfare rights activist whose work with the National Welfare Rights Organization greatly influenced the civil rights movement. Johnnie Tillmon, "Welfare Is a Women's Issue," *Ms. Magazine*, February 25, 2021, https://msmagazine.com/2021/03/25/welfare-is-a-womens-issue-ms-magazine-spring-1972/.

12. *Wyman v. James*, 400 U.S. 309 (1971).

13. Support Not Separation, https://supportnotseparation.blog; Global Women's Strike, https://globalwomenstrike.net/wagesforhousework.

14. "Remembering Michael Zinzun," Support Not Separation, *Diyzine*, n.d., https://diyzine.com/michaelzinzun.html.

15. Support Not Separation, https://sns-self-help-guide.net.

16. A New Way of Life, https://anewwayoflife.org.

17. Michael Fitzgerald, "New Bill Would Require States to Distinguish Poverty from Child Neglect," *The Imprint*, July 28, 2023, https://imprintnews.org/child-welfare-2/new-bill-would-require-states-to-distinguish-poverty-from-child-neglect/243316.

18. Elin Silverman, "Mothers Accused of Child Neglect Will Get Cash in D.C. Poverty Study," *Washington Post*, April 10, 2024, https://www.washingtonpost.com/dc-md-va/2024/04/10/child-neglect-cash-payments-dc-study.

Chapter 10. Change Everything? Notes on Abolitionist Strategies

1. Many of the ideas in this short chapter overlap with the thinking and words contained in *Abolition. Feminism. Now.*, which I coauthored with Angela Davis, Gina Dent, and Beth E. Richie. Their brilliance is seen throughout this work.

2. "Gov. JB Pritzker Announces Four-Year Plan to Transform Illinois Juvenile Justice System," CBS News, July 31, 2020, https://www.

cbsnews.com/chicago/news/gov-jb-pritzker-announces-four-year-plan-to-transform-illinois-juvenile-justice-system.

3. "Gov. Pritzker Announces New Community-Based Approach to Transform Juvenile Justice in Illinois," Press Release: Illinois Governor, July 31, 2020, https://www.illinois.gov/news/press-release.21879.html.

4. James Rainey and James Queally, "California Is Closing Its Last Youth Prisons. Will What Replaces Them Be Worse?," *Los Angeles Times,* June 2, 2023, https://www.latimes.com/california/story/2023-06-02/california-closing-youth-prisons-will-what-replaces-them-be-worse.

5. Rose Braz, "Kinder, Gentler, Gender Responsive Cages: Prison Expansion Is Not Prison Reform," *Women, Girls, and Criminal Justice* (October/November 2006): 87–91.

6. Audre Lorde, "Learning from the Sixties," address given at Harvard University celebration of Malcolm X, February 1982, https://www.blackpast.org/african-american-history/1982-audre-lorde-learning-60s/.

7. Cathy J. Cohen, "Punks, Bulldaggers, and Welfare Queens: The Radical Potential of Queer Politics?," *GLQ* 3, no. 4 (1997): 437–65.

8. Mari Matsuda, "Beside My Sister, Facing the Enemy: Legal Theory out of Coalition," 43 *Stanford Law Review* 43, no. 6 (1991): 1183, 1189. For more on Matsuda's question, see Angela Y. Davis et al., *Abolition. Feminism. Now.* (Chicago: Haymarket Books, 2022).

Chapter 13. Relationships, Not Reporting: The Transformative Justice Help Desk

1. Cara Page and Erica Woodland, eds., *Healing Justice Lineages: Dreaming at the Crossroads of Liberation, Collective Care, and Safety* (Oakland: AK Press, 2020); Shira Hassan, *Saving Our Own Lives: A Liberatory Practice of Harm Reduction* (Chicago: Haymarket Books, 2022).

2. Mia Mingus, "Transformative Justice: A Brief Description," *Leaving Evidence,* January 9, 2019, https://leavingevidence.wordpress.

com/2019/01/09/transformative-justice-a-brief-description.

3. Shira Hassan, *Saving Our Own Lives: A Liberatory Practice of Harm Reduction* (Chicago: Haymarket Books, 2022).

4. This is a statement created by and for the Young Women's Empowerment Project.

Chapter 15. Movement Building and the Experiment of Movement for Family Power

1. Described more fully below, the idea of a "movement winter" comes from Ayni Institute. "Movement Ecology," Ayni Institute, n.d., https://ayni.institute/movement-ecology-series.

2. "About," Movement for Family Power, https://www. movementforfamilypower.org/our-mission-and-approach.

3. Viola Castellano, "Walking a Fine Line: The Struggle for Parent Advocacy in the NYC Child Welfare System," *City and Society* 33, no. 5 (2021): 518–41, https://doi.org/10.1111/ciso.12416; "Rise Timeline," *Rise Magazine*, n.d., https://www.risemagazine.org/ timeline; Nikita Stewart, "A Fiji Junket, a Padlocked Office and a Pioneering Nonprofit's Collapse," *New York Times*, September 10, 2019, https://www.nytimes.com/2019/09/10/nyregion/child-welfare-nyc-.html; Martin Guggenheim et al., "Discovering Family Defense: A History of the Family Defense Clinic at New York University School of Law," *New York University Review of Law and Social Change* 41, no. 4 (2017): 539–68; Emma Ketteringham et al., "Healthy Mothers, Healthy Babies: A Reproductive Justice Response to the 'Womb-to-Foster-Care Pipeline,'" *City University of New York Law Review* 20, no. 1 (2016): 77–122, https://academicworks.cuny. edu/clr.

4. There are truly too many people to thank and name; however, there were some memorable conversations that were pivotal to the start of MFP, which include conversations with Dr. Lynn Roberts, Pilar Herrero, Farah Diaz Tello, Amanda Alexander, Marbre Stahly-Butts,

Mariame Kaba, C. Hope Tolliver, Erica Meiners, Dionna King, Andrea James, Andrea Ritchie, Dinah Ortiz, and so many others. In full transparency there are also some very important conversations we had with thought leaders that are not listed here, not because they were not critical to our work but because the relationships did not last for both Lisa and Erin. This happens in all spaces, including movement spaces. The tendency can be to erase those names as acknowledgments or decenter the influence of those conversations. We don't want to do that, but we do want to respect the ways that our relationships have shifted, our opinions on those influences, and the ways people wish to be represented in the story of MFP. For those reasons, those names are not listed, but we know the movement memory will keep those stories alive.

5. Robin Marty, "Victory for Purvi Patel, but Still a Loss for Reproductive Rights," *Truthout*, July 27, 2016, https://truthout.org/articles/victory-for-purvi-patel-but-still-a-loss-for-reproductive-rights; Fallon Speaker and Erin Miles Cloud, "When Child Welfare Intrusion Makes Reproductive Freedom an Illusion," *Urban Matters*, June 2, 2019, https://publicseminar.org/2019/06/when-child-welfare-intrusion-makes-reproductive-freedom-an-illusion.

6. "Soros Justice Fellowship," Open Society Foundations, n.d., https://www.opensocietyfoundations.org/grants/soros-justice-fellowships?past=1&page=3&fellow=lisa-sangoi&filter_past_year=2011%2C2009%2C2002%2C2013%2C2017.

7. Erin Miles Cloud et al., "Family Defense in the Age of Black Lives Matter," *City University of New York Law Review* 20, no. 1 (2020): 69–94, https://academicworks.cuny.edu/clr/vol20/iss1/14; Lisa Sangoi and Dorothy Roberts, "Black Families Matter: How the Child Welfare System Punishes Poor Families of Color," *The Appeal*, March 26, 2018, https://theappeal.org/black-families-matter-how-the-child-welfare-system-punishes-poor-families-of-color-33ad20e2882e.

8. Sade Daniels, "Black in Foster Care," *The Imprint*, July 15, 2016, https://imprintnews.org/blogger-co-op/

black-foster-youth-lives-matter/19569. "The same feelings of fear and anger that many in the black community have felt in response to the recent executions of unarmed black men by the police have had just as much of an impact on black foster youth, some of whom have had adverse experiences with the police. How telling is it of culturally competent and relevant practices that this isn't currently on our agenda? As a black child in foster care, I hated my blackness almost as much as I hated being in foster care because both seemed to make my life harder. As a black woman, studying and working within the foster care system, I'm finally beginning to see that my negative feelings about both may have been intertwined the whole time. #BlackFosterYouthLivesMatter."

It should be noted that there are now BLM chapters who explicitly center family policing, and family policing is incorporated into the Movement for Black Lives Vision for Black Lives Gender Justice demands. "Reimagine Child Safety," Black Lives Matter LA, accessed May 10, 2024, https://www.blmla.org/reimaginechildsafety; "Vision for Black Lives," Movement for Black Lives, accessed May 10, 2024, https://m4bl.org/policy-platforms.

9. We honor the bold critiques that existed that did not receive the platform they should have, such as those from Child Welfare Organizing project, Dorothy Roberts, and others.

10. Erica Meiners and Charity Tolliver, "Refusing to Be Complicit in Our Prison Nation: Teachers Rethinking Mandated Reporting," *Radical Teacher* 106 (November 2016), https://doi.org/10.5195/rt.2016.286.

11. If you are reading this and thinking to yourself that you want to support family policing organizers, but you don't know where their work is—we implore you to get out in your neighborhood, look at Facebook groups, check Reddit groups, Twitter, and so on. These were the things we did when we started MFP. We did not expect people to find us; we knew we had the obligation to seek out organizing, learn about it, and support it. It exists. We couldn't, and

you cannot, just simply rely on what is visible—or even what is most accessible. What is most visible is often what is most supported. It can be a good place to start, and maybe a good place to be organized into larger efforts. However, if you want to support the growth of a movement, keep reaching out, keep encouraging leadership, keep connecting, and most importantly keep going.

12. It should be noted that, again, this is also due to the fact there was a robust family defense movement in NYC, where Lisa and Erin worked for a good period of their career prior to starting MFP.

13. Diego Saavedra, "Building Narrative Power for Social Justice: Interview with Shanelle Matthews," *Midia and Cotidiano* 16, no. 3 (2022), https://periodicos.uff.br/midiaecotidiano/article/download/55518/32962.

14. "N'Tanya Lee: Grassroots Organizing Builds Power," YouTube, July 27, 2019, https://www.youtube.com/watch?v=Cnz5Wmb-oUg; "Momentum Webinar Series," YouTube, playlist, https://www.youtube.com/playlist?list=PLeJeAirMA52rCePt4WuuZPD1WXb2Jnd5H.

15. David S. Meyer and Steven A. Boutcher, "Signals and Spillover: *Brown v. Board of Education* and Other Social Movements," *Perspectives on Politics* 5, no. 1 (2007): 81–93, http://www.jstor.org/stable/20446351.

16. "Fiscal Sponsors Support Movements for Justice," Movement for Family Power, https://www.movementforfamilypower.org/resources.

17. Increasingly Black women, women of color, and leaders who understand the value of movement building and organizing and ground-softening work are moving into philanthropy and grasstops work, and their support was essential to MFP starting and becoming sustainable.

18. "Movement Ecology," Ayni Institute.

19. The National Council, https://www.nationalcouncil.us.

20. Repeal ASFA, https://www.repealasfa.org.

21. NY Informed Consent, https://www.informedconsentny.com.

22. "CAIP," https://www.caip.us/ourpeople; "Shanelle Matthews," City College, https://www.ccny.cuny.edu/profiles/shanelle-matthews;

"Elizabeth Dawes Gay," *Rewire*, https://rewirenewsgroup.com/authors/elizabeth-dawes-gay.

23. A special acknowledgment to Miriam Mack and Jasmine Wali and to all of the coalition members that can be found at "Our Coalition," NY Informed Consent, https://www.informedconsentny.com/our-coalition.

24. "Movement Seasons," YouTube, https://www.youtube.com/watch?v=KSwnVINjYgI.

25. Shin Imai, "A Counter-Pedagogy for Social Justice, Core Skills for Community-Based Lawyering," *Clinical Law Review* 9, no. 1 (2002): 195.

26. Paul Engler et al., *Funding Social Movements, How Mass Protest Makes an Impact*, Ayni Institute, May 2018, available at https://files.elfsightcdn.com/eafe4a4d-3436-495d-b748-5bdce62d911d/b8031dc9-055a-4c64-9b90-c1b843b27df4/Funding-Social-Movements-Guide.pdf. See also Sean Dobson, *Freedom Funders: Philanthropy and the Civil Rights Movement 1955–1965*, National Committee for Responsive Philanthropy, June 2014, https://ncrp.org/wp-content/uploads/2016/11/Freedom_Funders_and_the_Civil_Rights_Movement-FINAL.pdf.

27. Mark Engler and Paul Engler, *This Is an Uprising* (New York: Nation Books, 2016); Barbara Ransby, *Ella Baker and the Black Freedom Movement: A Radical Democratic Vision* (Chapel Hill, NC: University of North Carolina Press, 2003); Frances Piven and Richard Cloward, *Poor People's Movements: Why They Succeed and How They Fail* (New York: Vintage, 1979).

28. Ayni Institute, "Movements and Leaders Have Seasons—It's Important to Know Which One You Are In," *Medium*, January 25, 2022, https://medium.com/@ayni.institute/movements-and-leaders-have-seasons-its-important-to-know-which-one-you-are-in-c5dbaa2c37ad.

29. We write this acknowledging that what is abolitionist versus reformist work is not always clear and that this analysis is constantly expanding over time. We know that sometimes we intend to do abolitionist

work and later know that it was reform work and vice versa—we get that. This is about the times people know that the work is clearly not abolitionist.

30. The Possible Lab, https://www.theposslab.com.

Appendix

1. Laura Chow Reeve, Shawn Koyano, Shannon Perez-Darby, *You Matter: An Illustrated Guide for Young People Beyond Mandatory Reporting*, Mandatory Reporting Is Not Neutral, https://www. mandatoryreportingisnotneutral.com/zine.

Index

Page numbers in **bold** indicate illustrations.

Downstate Medical Center in
    Brooklyn, 124
Du Bois, W. E. B., 152
Duggan, Sarah (developing art work
    for "Breaking Silos in Reproductive
    Justice" symposium, **172**

economy building, 217–18
ELL. *See* English-language learner
Elzarka, Noran, 164–75
English-language learner, 194, 197
Erazo, Mar (developing art for "Spot
    the Difference"), **53**
"Everyday People Build Extra Ordinary
    Possibilities: Parental Organizing
    as Key to Ending Family Policing"
    (Koyano), 192–201

Faboo Listserv for New York City, 101
families
    defining, 56–70
    postcolonial family structures,
        61–62, 69
    prioritizing child protection over
        family preservation, 91–92
    redefining family, 68–69
    Rivera's experiences, 56–59, 62–63,
        69–70
    violence in, 49–51, 56–70
family policing system (FPS), 7–10, 54
    abolitionist strategies to use against,
        148–59
    building solidarity to end, 172,
        174–75
    costs of, 8
    designed to isolate people, 171
    and the ending of mandated
        reporting, 102, 182–84
    impact of on the family, Rivera's

experiences, 56–70
liberatory harm reduction helping to
    end, 179–82
Mandated Reporters Against
    Mandated Reporting organizing
    against, 99–121
and Movement for Black Lives, 43,
    45
Movement for Family Power
    organizing against, 202–26
origins of the term "family police,"
    15–25
parental organizing to end, 192–201
"Prevention, Reparations, and
    Reunification: Black Families
    and Healing the Harms of Family
    Policing" (lake), 35–45
protecting youth from, 46–55
racial dimensions of, 85–95
relationship to prison industrial
    complex, 10, 16–17, 149, 182
reproductive rights movement
    leaving behind, 166
role of TJ Help Desk, 176–91
safety requiring the need to
    dismantle, 26–34
ways to organize against, 122–47
See also mandatory reporting of
    domestic and sexual violence
family separation, 43, 46, 78–80, 90,
    94, 105, 129, 162
    experiences of Corey Best, 27,
        33–34
    experiences of jaboa lake and her
        sisters, 35–45
    experiences of zara raven, 46–49
    and forced birth, 168–69
    forced, 168
    harms caused by, 22–23, 43, 105

Index 273

Contributors

Corey B. Best is a Black father, community organizer and activist. Originally from Washington, DC, Corey now resides in Florida. Corey founded Mining for Gold (MFG) in 2020. The idea for MFG is directly influenced by the 405 years of racialized arrangement in our communities, and that we all have pieces of metaphorical gold flowing within us. MFG's vision is to actualize a society where we flourish without racialized oppression and carceral restrictions to reclaiming humanity. Corey has attached himself to "justice doing"— a movement and never-ending journey guided by the principled struggle to abolish family policing and all carceral systems. Corey brings a deepened historical and contemporary analysis of the invention of race, racism, systems of oppression, and how those systems interconnect to produce white advantage gaps. As a practice and a discipline, Corey dreams of new worlds of freedom, while practicing abolitionism through movement organizing, reflecting his membership on the advisory board of Movement for Family Power, and his membership in the Repeal CAPTA work group. In 2019, in partnership with leaders, communities, and parents, Corey curated the Authentic Family Engagement and Strengthening approach and, in 2021, coauthored the article "Authentic Family Engagement and Strengthening Approach: A Promising Family-Centered Approach for Advancing Racial Justice with Families Involved with the Child Protection System" (*Journal of Justice-Informed Social Work Practice and Research*). In 2023, Corey coauthored the introduction of NACC's fourth-edition Red Book. In 2024, Corey coauthored the published research article "Evaluating the Authentic Family Engagement and Strengthening Approach" (*Journal of Justice-Informed Social Work Practice and Research*).

Reverend Annie Chambers is a lifelong grassroots community activist fighting against poverty and for universal basic income, housing, welfare, and health care rights. She is a founding member and past president of the Baltimore Welfare Rights Union and cochair of the National Welfare Rights Union. A Black mother/grandmother/ great-grandmother from inner-city Baltimore, Chambers was the past director of Big Momma's House, which provides daytime shelter for children, feeds homeless people, works with drug-addicted parents, and helps families with children find permanent shelter. She is also the former RAB program representative for Douglass Homes Public Housing in Baltimore. Today she runs a food and household goods giveaway program on Baltimore's East Side. And she still fights for the poor, working class, and oppressed all over the world.

Erin Miles Cloud is a civil rights attorney. She is the cofounder of Movement for Family Power, and a former family defense public defender. She is a Black, mixed-race mother of two beautiful children.

Noran Elzarka is helpline counsel at If/When/How, where she is working to assist individuals seeking support and information around reproductive justice. Prior to joining If/When/How, Noran began her legal career as a public defender in 2018 at Brooklyn Defender Services in the Family Defense Practice representing parents and families who were impacted by the family regulation system. Noran attended and graduated from CUNY School of Law where she worked with CLEAR to counter post-9/11 policies and practices that have particularly affected Muslim, Arab, South Asian, and other communities in NYC and facilitated numerous Know Your Rights workshops. Noran was also active with the National Lawyers Guild's Parole Preparation Project, collaborating with and advocating for people eligible for parole who are serving indeterminate sentences in New York State prisons. Noran is committed to working toward the abolition of violent systems that continue to intervene and oppress Black and brown communities and dreams of a world where people can make decisions for themselves and their families without state intervention.

Brianna Harvey is a scholar, practitioner, and assistant professor in the Department of Sociology at California State University, Fullerton. Her interdisciplinary research examines the ways carceral systems utilize policies, practices, and other mechanisms of control to perpetuate anti-Blackness and impact the lives of Black youth and their families. Dr. Harvey's most recent publication is entitled "'Ain't Nobody About to Trap Me': The Violence of Multi-System Collusion and Entrapment for Incarcerated Disabled Girls of Color" and was published in the *Journal of School Violence*. She received her PhD in education from the University of California, Los Angeles, and her master of social work degree from the University of Southern California.

Shira Hassan is the former executive director of the Young Women's Empowerment Project, an organizing project led by and for young people that have current or former experience in the sex trade and street economies. A lifelong harm reductionist and prison abolitionist, she is a cofounder of Justice Practice Collaborative, a capacity-building project for organizations and community members working at the intersection of transformative justice, harm reduction, and collective liberation. Shira is the coauthor of *Fumbling Towards Repair: A Workbook for Community Accountability Facilitators* (AK Press, 2019) and the author of *Saving Our Own Lives: A Liberatory Practice of Harm Reduction* (Haymarket Books, 2022).

Shawn Koyano is a Black queer mother, survivor, and advocate for families seeking community, belonging, and healing from violent systems. She strives to center and ground her work in Black feminist radical care, abolition, and dreaming of possibilities for families to be safe and whole. She is a member of Mandatory Reporting Is Not Neutral (MRNN), Collective Justice, and API Chaya's Queer Network Program and does her work on the unceded ancestral lands of the Duwamish people.

jaboa lake is an auntie, sister, liberation researcher, and organizer. jaboa is a cofounder of the sunsetted Black Lives Matter Portland, and the last fifteen years of jaboa's work has centered liberation of oppressed people and solidarity across movements through using research as a tactic within grassroots strategies, removing the collateral consequences of criminalization, youth and adult political education, craft and cultural organizing, and cultivating Black joy.

Elizabeth Ling is the senior helpline counsel at If/When/How, where she manages the Repro Legal Helpline, assisting people in understanding the laws around a variety of reproductive experiences, including self-managed abortion, youth access to abortion, and birth justice. Prior to joining If/When/How, Elizabeth was senior program manager of Criminal Defense Initiatives at the Center for Court Innovation, where she provided research-driven technical assistance aimed at improving access to and quality of indigent defense representation across the country. Elizabeth began her career as a family defense attorney with Brooklyn Defender Services, representing parents facing allegations of abuse or neglect and helping them to reunite or keep their families together.

Erica R. Meiners is a writer, organizer and educator in Chicago. Proud uncty of many, and a lover of bees and cats and long-distance running, Erica collaboratively ran a number of initiatives—including the Prison Neighborhood Arts/Education Project. They are the co-author of *Abolition. Feminism. Now.* (Haymarket Books, 2022) and *The Feminist and the Sex Offender: Confronting Sexual Harm and Ending State Violence* (Verso Books, 2020).

Shannon Perez-Darby is a queer, mixed-race Latina, founding member of the Accountable Communities Consortium, and a core member of the Mandatory Reporting Is Not Neutral project. Centering queer and trans communities of color, Shannon Perez-Darby works to create the conditions to support loving, equitable relationships and communities while focusing on issues of domestic and sexual violence, accountability, and abolition.

Leah Plasse is a born and raised New Yorker and school social worker with over thirteen years of experience. In addition to her day job, Leah facilitates anti-oppressive workshops for clinicians and has been an activist organizing since she was a teenager. She is invested in un/learning the multitude of ways social work upholds white supremacy and reinforces oppressive systems. Leah cofounded and co-facilitates the Mandated Reporters Against Mandated Reporting group. She practices from an intersectional, anti–oppressive systems perspective that centers holistic community healing. Leah is a co-author of a new *Culturally Responsive Inventory for Clinicians on an Anti-Oppressive Journey* (2023).

Margaret Prescod is a cofounder of Black Women for Wages for Housework, coordinator of Women of Color in the Global Women's Strike, and joint coordinator of the Care Income Now campaign. She is on the board of the National Welfare Rights Union. She is founder of the Black Coalition Fighting Back Serial Murders and is the host of *Sojourner Truth*, a nationally syndicated show on Pacifica Radio. She is a mother and the author of *Black Women Bringing It All Back Home* (Falling Wall Press, 1980).

zara raven is a Black Caribbean Mad queer mama, educator, and organizer. zara is a coordinator of the Philly Childcare Collective, working to support intergenerational movements, and the codirector of the Safer Movements Collective, a healing justice organization nurturing the wellness and relational skills of people invested in liberation. zara is also the former coordinator of Queenie's Crew at Project NIA, a program that engaged children in learning to build communities of care without prisons or policing. zara also organized to end the criminalization of sex workers with Decrim-Now DC and Decrim NY.

Ignacio G. Hutía Xeiti Rivera is a cultural sociologist with expertise in sexual trauma, healing, and liberation for marginalized people. They are an internationally known gender-nonconforming speaker, trainer, and consultant. Ignacio is the founder and co–executive director of the HEAL Project.

Dorothy Roberts is the fourteenth Penn Integrates Knowledge Professor, the George A. Weiss University Professor of Law and Sociology, and the Raymond Pace and Sadie Tanner Mossell Alexander Professor of Civil Rights at University of Pennsylvania. She is also the founding director of the Penn Program on Race, Science, and Society. An internationally acclaimed scholar, activist, and social critic, she has written and lectured extensively on the interplay of gender, race, and class in legal issues concerning reproduction, bioethics, and child welfare.

Arneta Rogers is the executive director of the Center on Reproductive Rights and Justice (CRRJ) at Berkeley Law. They are an Oakland-based Black queer feminist, advocate, and movement lawyer with over a decade of experience of fighting for racial and reproductive justice. They previously led the gender, sexuality, and reproductive justice program at the ACLU of Northern California, where their work focused on the intersections of criminalization and reproductive justice. They also served as the policy director of Positive Women's Network–USA. Arneta has worked on campaigns to ensure the right to bodily autonomy and access to reproductive and pregnancy-related care for incarcerated people, to modernize California's discriminatory HIV criminalization laws, and to decriminalize loitering for sex work. They were a 2022 Law for Black Lives Movement Lawyering fellow and Rockwood Leadership Institute Reproductive Health, Rights, and Justice fellow. Arneta graduated from University of California Law, San Francisco, in the social justice concentration. They enjoy spending time in nature with their kid, playing basketball, and drumming in the streets for the movement.

Lisa Sangoi is committed to working in service of reproductive justice, having spent the past decade-plus advocating against the separation of children and families through the child welfare and foster system. She has participated in or co-led several advocacy and organizing campaigns to roll back laws, policies, and practices that punish mamas for exercising their reproductive decision making. She has also had the privilege of providing legal representation to women targeted by the child welfare and criminal legal systems through trial and appellate advocacy. She spends quite a bit of time learning about drug use, pregnancy, and parenting, and she regularly consults on related child welfare cases and legislation throughout the country. Her writing has been published in academic journals, print media, and advocacy reports, and she presents often on these injustices. She founded and codirected Movement for Family Power, an organization that uses movement lawyering to support grassroots organizing around foster system reform and abolition. She has previously worked at Mothers Outreach Network, NYU Law Family Defense Clinic, National Advocates for Pregnant Women, Women Prison Association Incarcerated Mothers Law Project, and Brooklyn Defender Services Family

Defense Practice. She is the proud mother of two lovely children, and in a former life, she was a dancer and violinist.

jasmine Sankofa is the executive director of Movement for Family Power and is a passionate movement lawyer, scholar, activist, storyteller, birth worker, and bonus/god mama, jasmine is committed to abolition and grounded in the belief that when we fight, we win. Her work has focused on sex work decriminalization, decarceration, survivor justice, and ending forced family separations, centering the voices and lived experiences of Black women and girls.

Kylee Sunderlin is the legal services director at If/When/How, where she oversees the provision of legal services through the Repro Legal Helpline, as well as the enhancement of technical assistance and public education to allied organizations and health care providers. Prior to joining If/When/How, Kylee was a family defense attorney at Brooklyn Defender Services, where she represented parents facing allegations of abuse or neglect and experiencing inhumane family separation. She was also a Soros Justice Fellow at National Advocates for Pregnant Women with a project that combined litigation, public education, and advocacy to challenge interventions by the family regulation system in response to medication-assisted treatment.

C. Hope Tolliver is the founder and director of Black on Both Sides. The former director of organizing for one of the largest and oldest organizing groups in Chicago, Southwest Youth Collaborative, C. Hope is a mother and an artist.

Jasmine Wali is a writer, organizer, and strategic policy consultant. She partners with national policy, movement building, health care, and community organizations and institutions on initiatives to end the criminalization of parents and families—particularly parents who use drugs and survivors of gender-based violence. Jasmine has been instrumental in scaling up the capacity of grassroots organizations working toward abolishing family policing. She has also supported legislative advocacy in three states to limit the scope of mandated reporting, and co-led the writing and implementation of a "mandated supporting" curriculum for social work students. Jasmine has spoken about family policing and mandated reporting at a number of congressional briefings, state hearings, colleges, conferences, and community events, and she has written for *The Nation*, *Boston Globe*, *Columbia Social Work Review*, *CUNY Law Review*, *CUNY Theory, Research, and Action in Urban Education Journal*, and more.

Amanda Wallace founded Operation Stop CPS in May 2021. Operation Stop CPS is a grassroots campaign that works with families and community partners to resist local child welfare agencies. Amanda coauthored *The Respond in Power Guide* (2021), a guide that parents and caretakers can use when engaging with the system. Amanda also cochairs the Black Mothers March on the White House coalition, which held its first mobilization in Washington, DC, in 2022.

Eleni Zimiles is a social worker grounded at the cross section of healing, education, and organizing. Her work strives to build authentic community, foster creativity and critical consciousness, and disrupt harmful relationships and systems of power.

About Haymarket Books

Haymarket Books is a radical, independent, nonprofit book publisher based in Chicago. Our mission is to publish books that contribute to struggles for social and economic justice. We strive to make our books a vibrant and organic part of social movements and the education and development of a critical, engaged, and internationalist left.

We take inspiration and courage from our namesakes, the Haymarket Martyrs, who gave their lives fighting for a better world. Their 1886 struggle for the eight-hour day—which gave us May Day, the international workers' holiday—reminds workers around the world that ordinary people can organize and struggle for their own liberation. These struggles—against oppression, exploitation, environmental devastation, and war—continue today across the globe.

Since our founding in 2001, Haymarket has published more than nine hundred titles. Radically independent, we seek to drive a wedge into the risk-averse world of corporate book publishing. Our authors include Angela Y. Davis, Arundhati Roy, Keeanga-Yamahtta Taylor, Eve Ewing, Aja Monet, Mariame Kaba, Naomi Klein, Rebecca Solnit, Olúfẹ́mi O. Táíwò, Mohammed El-Kurd, José Olivarez, Noam Chomsky, Winona LaDuke, Robyn Maynard, Leanne Betasamosake Simpson, Howard Zinn, Mike Davis, Marc Lamont Hill, Dave Zirin, Astra Taylor, and Amy Goodman, among many other leading writers of our time. We are also the trade publishers of the acclaimed Historical Materialism Book Series.

Haymarket also manages a vibrant community organizing and event space in Chicago, Haymarket House, the popular Haymarket Books Live event series and podcast, and the annual Socialism Conference.

Also Available from Haymarket Books

No Cop City, No Cop World
Lessons from the Movement
Edited by Kamau Franklin, Micah Herskind, and Mariah Parker

Skyscraper Jails
The Abolitionist Fight Against Jail Expansion in New York City
Zhandarka Kurti and Jarrod Shanahan

Abolition and Social Work
Possibilities, Paradoxes, and the Practice of Community Care
Edited by Mimi E. Kim, Cameron Rasmussen, and Durrell M. Washington
Foreword by Mariame Kaba

Defund
Conversations Toward Abolition
by Calvin John Smiley

Let This Radicalize You
Organizing and the Revolution of Reciprocal Care
by Kelly Hayes and Mariame Kaba

Abolition Feminisms
Organizing, Survival, and Transformative Practice
Edited by Alisa Bierria, Jakeya Caruthers, and Brooke Lober
Foreword by Dean Spade